MARTIN BUBER

by Charlie May Simon

MARTIN · *Wisdom in*
BUBER · *Our Time*
THE STORY OF AN OUTSTANDING
JEWISH THINKER AND HUMANIST

by Charlie May Simon

E. P. DUTTON & CO., INC., NEW YORK

First Edition

Published simultaneously in Canada by
Clarke, Irwin & Company Limited, Toronto and Vancouver

Library of Congress Catalog Card Number: 74-81724

C64410/11   [04]

Grateful acknowledgment is made for permission to use the
following copyrighted material:

Simon & Schuster for the poem by Martin Buber on page 73
from *A Believing Humanism*. Copyright © 1967
by Maurice Friedman.

Charles Scribner's Sons and T. T. Clark, Edinburgh, for
quotations from *I and Thou* by Martin Buber. Copyright © 1958
Charles Scribner's Sons.

Schocken Books Inc. for the poem on page 118 from
Franz Rosenzweig: His Life and Thought, edited by
Nahum N. Glatzer. Copyright © 1953, 1961 by Schocken
Books Inc.

The photograph on page 162 was presented to the Library
of the Jewish Theological Seminary of America in New York
by Dr. Simon Greenberg. It is used here with the Library's
kind permission.

TO THE BEST OF FRIENDS
Mary and Booker Worthen

CONTENTS

8   CONTENTS

ILLUSTRATIONS

MARTIN BUBER

1 BOYHOOD IN LEMBERG

ADELE BUBER, LOOKING DOWN AT HER SMALL GRANDSON, MUST OFTEN HAVE WONDERED WHAT THOUGHTS LAY BEHIND THOSE dark, questioning eyes. A child's memories are fleeting, like the sunbeams that dance in and out of his reach, a brief flash of sound or sensation. There may have been strains of a lullaby faintly recalled, the warmth of a caress, a gentle face bending over the cradle and a tear that fell. After that, fear and loneliness, and the comforting grasp of a father's hand.

Martin Buber was not quite three when, in 1880, his parents were divorced. His father brought him from Vienna, his birthplace, to live with his grandparents

Solomon and Adele Buber in Lemberg. Here he could grow up in the same pious atmosphere the father had known as a child.

Lemberg, in the province of Galicia, was then a part of the great Austrian Empire under Francis Joseph. The whole province lies on the northern slopes of the Carpathian Mountains, exposed to the cold winds blowing down from the Russian plains, and shut off from the warmth of the south. The winters there are long, and the snow lies deep almost half the year, but Galicia's fertile valleys and rich grainfields have been coveted by one country after another since the province was an independent kingdom eight hundred years ago. The Tatars and Huns had fought over it long before that; then came the Hungarians, Lithuanians, and Turks. Charles XII captured the land for Sweden in 1704. Four times it became part of Poland; three times it was Russian; and twice it had belonged to Austria.

The name of the principal city had been changed each time it was conquered, from Leopolis, meaning City of Lions, to the Russian Lvov, the Polish Lwow, and now the Austrian Lemberg. The roads leading to the city had been tramped down by many generations of footsteps and horses' hoofs, and the wheels or runners of stagecoaches, carriages, sleighs, and heavy rumbling carts. Pilgrims had come this way, and monks, their faces half hidden by cowls. There had been troops of actors, acrobats, and pantomimists, troubadours and bands of wandering scholars singing their rowdy songs. Tradesmen had come bent under the weight of knapsacks, and peddlers pushing barrows of goods to sell. Soldiers, too, had come marching through from one or another of the four directions. Every inch of the road had been fought over, with so much blood spilled that it had become known as the Dark Trail. And in the wake of battle came groups of men with their families, driven from their homes and searching for a place where they could live their own lives and worship in their own way, unharmed and at peace. Here in Galicia they formed communities, built their houses of worship, and organized schools for their young so that the knowledge and wisdom of their ancient past could be carried on through the generations to come.

Solomon Buber was a well-respected member of such a community in Lemberg. He was a wealthy banker, and at the same time a brilliant scholar of classic Hebrew. He spoke the language as it had been spoken in biblical times. With his dark beard beginning to turn gray, a black cap covering his head and a fringed prayer shawl around his shoulders, he was like a patriarch of old, dignified, yet with the humility of one who feels himself at all times in the presence of the Divine. Over the doorway of both his town and country house was a small case-enclosed scroll with holy words written on it, a reminder to keep the commandments, the first moral laws given to man. Before entering the door each time he returned home, he put a finger reverently to the scroll, then touched the finger to his lips. When he removed his hat, he put on a tight-fitting black skullcap to wear inside the house, for the head must never be bared in the presence of God, and to him God was present everywhere.

Martin grew up supremely loved and protected in this household of piety and affection. Here in this sanctuary where no harm could reach him, the loneliness and indefinitely felt sorrows of his early childhood faded until they had no more reality than a dimly remembered dream. The customs and the prayers that he learned gave him a sense of feeling part of the distant past of his ancestors, linked with the present and with a future stretching on to eternity.

"Hear, O Israel, the Lord our God, the Lord is One."

There were prayers and religious laws that governed even a small boy from the time he woke up in the morning until he went to sleep at night:

"As soon as there is light enough to recognize a familiar face at a distance of four cubits, it is time for the morning prayer.

"It is unlawful for us to go the distance of four cubits from our bed without washing the hands. It is incumbent upon us immediately after rising to perform our ablution."

It became as much a habit as breathing, or sleeping and waking, for Martin, as soon as he got out of bed in the morning, to pour water from the pitcher three times over his right hand up to the wrist, and three times over the left. Before drying them he intoned the child's prayer of early morning, in the language of the prophets as his grandfather had taught him:

" 'Blessed art Thou, the Eternal our God, the King of

the Universe, who hath sanctified us with His commandments and commanded us to wash the hands.' "

He was told: "Pronounce each word distinctly, and when you say 'the Lord is One,' dwell upon the word *One,* so the unity of the Eternal will be fixed upon your mind."

In the stories told or read to a child there was always a reminder of the Divine, though the meaning could sometimes be puzzling. *Outside the gates of Rome there sits a leprous beggar, waiting. He is the Messiah.* "What is he waiting for?" Martin wanted to know. The answer was "He waits for you." It was long before he understood.

His grandmother told him stories from the religious books, the Talmud and the Kabbala, as she had heard them in her childhood:

"There was once a king who was driven off his throne and had to flee to the wilderness. A demon sat on the throne in his place, dressed in the royal robes. He was so much like the king in looks and manner that the people thought he was the king. But no matter what disguise the devil takes, he can never stop being a devil."

Martin listened intently as the grandmother went on with her story about the devil's reign of cruelty. The people were so abused and so heavily burdened that they could bear it no longer, and they rose up in revolt. Martin pondered over this for a long time. Why hadn't the king's subjects realized that only a devil could behave in such a way? Why hadn't they recognized him for what he was and gone off in search of their true king?

His grandmother had her own way of speaking German, and through her Martin learned to love the beauty of the language. German was not spoken in the ghetto where she had grown up, and German books were forbidden as worldly. When she was fifteen she managed to come into possession of a few; these she treasured and kept hidden in a storehouse. There, in semidarkness, she spent many an hour reading them, delighting in each word and phrase.

From his scholarly grandfather Martin learned the classic Hebrew, not only the prayers and Psalms he chanted but the written word as well. There were twenty-two letters of the Hebrew alphabet, all consonants, which he had to learn. And he had to know how, without vowels, the position of the letters gave the word its sound. There were also punctuation marks that were important to learn, marks that could change the pronunciation or the meaning of a word. Martin discovered that the smallest one, no more than a dot, was called a *yood*. When two of these were placed one above the other, it signified a pause; but when two were placed side by side, it meant the name of God.

"When God was about to create the world by His word, the twenty-two letters of the alphabet descended from His terrible and august crown whereon they were engraved. They stood around God and, one after the other, they spoke and entreated, 'Create the world through me.' "

Martin practiced forming the letters in his copybook, going from right to left. In the story from the Book of

Splendor, one of the sacred books written a thousand years ago, the first letter to step forward with its claim was ת , pronounced *taw*.

"O Lord of the world! May it be your will to create the world through me, seeing that through me you will give the Torah to Israel by the hand of Moses." The Holy One, blessed be He, made answer and said, "No.' " "Why not?" asked taw. "Because," God answered, "in days to come I shall place you as a sign of death on the forehead of men."

Martin formed the letters that had stepped forward, each with its claim to help create the world. The letter ש , called *shin,* is the initial of *Shaddai,* one of the names for God, but it is also the initial for *sheker,* falsehood. פ is used in *Podeh,* the word for Redeemer, and it is used for *peshah,* meaning transgression. מ is the beginning of *Melsk,* King, one of the titles for God, and it is the beginning of *mehumah,* confusion.

"O Lord may it be your will to begin the creation with me," said the letter that is the initial for *samek,* which means the upholder of all that fall. But God said, "You are needed in the place where you are. You must continue to uphold all that fall."

All the letters had been rejected for one reason or another except one, when God turned to ב *bet.* It is through this letter that all praises to God are made, for it is said, "Blessed (*Baruch*) be the Lord forever, Amen and Amen." God said to *bet,* "Blessed be he that comes in the name of the Lord." And so it is that *Bereskit* (in the beginning) God created the heavens and the earth.

Solomon Buber felt, with some other Hebrew scholars of his time, that the language should not be confined to ancient sacred writings alone. He read the works of Molière, Goethe, Shakespeare, and Homer, translated in Hebrew, and did some translating of his own from modern German writings. With both Solomon and Adele Buber as teachers, Martin's education was a well-rounded one.

The boys of the neighborhood attended school in a room set aside for that purpose in one of the synagogues. Six days a week, from early morning until late evening, they sat on plain wooden benches facing the teacher, reciting in unison one and another of the 613 commandments handed down from Moses. Their heads, covered with black skullcaps, were bent low over their books, and their bodies swayed to and fro in rhythm with the words. The boys had no other book to study but the Torah. This was enough, the elders said, for the Torah, which God Himself learns anew day after day, contains all one ever needs to know.

Martin was never to forget the confusion of languages he heard in his childhood. Polish was still spoken in the streets and schools of Lemberg, but in his father's and grandfather's house he heard German. In the Jewish neighborhoods there was the rough and tender sound of Yiddish, and from the synagogues came the deep, sonorous chant of ancient Hebrew.

The peasants living near Solomon Buber's summer estate at Sadagora and those who came to the city on market day greeted one another with the words "May

*Polish Jews of about the time Martin Buber was
a boy in Lemberg.* (CULVER PICTURES, INC.)

Jesus Christ be praised," and the answer came, "Forever and ever." And in the streets close to the synagogues men greeted each other with "Peace be with you."

Street sounds floated up to the room where Martin studied his lessons: the click of footsteps, the tramp of horses' hoofs, the rattle of cart or carriage wheels on cobblestones. Children too young for school shouted in their play, and housewives gossiped as they drew water from the town pump. But from sunset on Friday until evening of the following day, there was a hushed atmosphere. Sometimes a dog barked from far away, and another answered as a matter of principle. In winter the wind whistled through the narrow streets, and on a warm day of spring a sparrow broke the silence with its song. But there was no sound of horse or vehicle. All shops and stores were closed, and no smoke rose from the kitchens of houses.

The Sabbath was a day of holy rest, of tranquillity and gladness. The grandmother and the servant girls prepared for it well in advance every week. The house was made spotlessly clean, and food was cooked to last until the fires could be lighted again at the Sabbath's end. There must be enough in the cupboards for the family, for possible visitors or a stranger passing that way, and for any that were so poor they could not afford white flour for the Sabbath bread.

When the sun was low and shadows were long, the grandmother, fresh from the ceremonial bath, put on her black silk dress, and covered her head with her finest shawl. She lighted the candles on the dining table. There were two candles, a reminder of the words *remember* and *observe*. The silver sparkled in the glow of the flame, and the linen cloth stood out white and pure. The table was set as if for a feast, and at the same time it was something of an altar, signifying holiness in even the simple acts of life. The grandmother bowed her head and stretched out her arms toward the candles, saying the prayer of lighting the Sabbath lights. When the last rays of the sun disappeared behind the roof-tops, Martin and his grandparents greeted one another, chanting together, "Peace be unto you, angels of peace."

"Her children rise up and call her blessed; her husband also, he praises her." The grandfather turned to his wife with an affectionate smile as he quoted the words of Solomon to her. "Many daughters have done virtuously, but you excel them all."

A silver pitcher and bowl were brought out and passed around for the ceremony of washing the hands. The grandfather then poured wine into a silver goblet, blessed it, took a sip, and passed it to the others at the table. He blessed the Sabbath bread, broke it, and passed that also.

> "When you eat of the labor of your hands,
> Happy shall you be, and it shall be well with you."

Every week there was this same holiday spirit, a blending of joy and holiness, a sense of unity of the human with the Divine. The talk at the table was cheerful, for on this day there must be no mean or gloomy thoughts, no sadness and no sighing. Table songs were sung, praising the beautiful and holy Sabbath day, and telling of the weary who found rest from their labors. Biblical quotations about this day God gave to man were chanted.

"The higher soul descends into men on the Sabbath," a wise rabbi had said. No man was too poor to celebrate, even down to the humblest ragpicker or dealer in secondhand clothes, or the beggar in the street. They came from the ceremonial bath clean and glowing as if all trouble and sorrow had been washed away. Their children were dressed in the best they could afford, little girls in pretty frocks with sashes and bows, and boys in clean, neatly pressed jackets and trousers.

Solomon Buber preferred the small neighborhood synagogues, where humble men met and worshiped, to the fashionable ones of the city. His prayer book was old, and full of mystical directions.

"O Lord, guard my tongue from evil and my lips from guile, and to those who slander me, may I give no heed."

Martin attended the synagogue with his grandfather, standing beside him facing east, the direction of the altar, while the cantor chanted the eighteen blessings. Every week the great scroll was taken out of its embroidered mantle, and one or another of the men in the congregation was called up to read a passage from the five books of Moses. Solomon Buber took part in those readings, holding in his hand the pointed wand to indi-

*Two modern-day Jewish men at prayer. They wear the tra-
ditional fringed prayer shawl, and one reads from the sacred book.* (CULVER PICTURES, INC.)

cate the place, for it was forbidden to touch the inside of the scroll with the bare hand. Martin listened silently, and every word of the ancient tongue penetrated into his heart. All about him were pious, bearded men with heads covered and shoulders wrapped in fringed prayer shawls. Their bodies solemnly swayed to the chanting of the familiar words. For countless generations every line and every word of the Torah had been discussed and argued over and written about.

In the village of Sadagora, close to the Buber estate where the family spent the summers, the worshipers were still more fervent. Their relationship with God went beyond rituals, beyond words written in a scroll or some old and musty book. They felt God's presence everywhere and at all times, in every thought and action. They made their religion one of joy and praise. They danced in the synagogue as a way of giving thanks, accompanied by phrases they chanted from the Psalms:

" 'The little hills rejoice on every side. The pastures are clothed with flocks; the valleys are also covered over with corn. They shout for joy; they also sing.' "

Their heads were covered with round black hats, or hats like turbans, bordered with brown fur. On each side of their bearded faces a long curl hung from the temple, bobbing and swaying with their movements. They were dressed alike, in high boots and long black coats, but the clothes of some were of fine cloth, while those of others were cheap and rusty from long wear. There were tailors among them whose days were spent cross-legged on a table, bent over needle and cloth. There were peddlers, draymen, day laborers, tenant farmers, Talmudic scholars, wan-faced from long hours of study, teachers, merchants, bankers. All were considered equal, high and low, rich and poor, for when one loves God, they said, one loves all His creation. As they stamped and danced about the room in holy ecstasy, hands on one another's shoulders, one would begin another verse of the Psalms. All the others took it up, chanting as in one deep, booming voice, their steps keeping time to the song. They sang of mountains that skipped like rams and little hills like lambs. They called on the heavens to rejoice and the earth to be glad, the fields and all the trees to rejoice also.

In a quieter mood the men told tales of their past leaders. Some were so saintly, they said, that they could remember the time before they were born, and they knew the future as well as they knew their own heartbeat. They could look from one end of the earth to the other, and were aware of everything that happened, as if it were happening inside their own bodies. The men talked also of the leaders then living. There was Rabbi David Moshe from the nearby village of Tchortkov, a man tender and humane to all creatures. Once, it was said, when he opened the Book of Psalms and began to recite the praises, God called down to him: "David Moshe, my son, I am putting the whole world in your hands. Now do with it just as you like."

"Oh, if he'd only given me the world," said David Moshe's brother, "I'd know very well what to do with it.

But David Moshe is so faithful a servant that when he gives the world back it is exactly as it was when he received it."

Men like Martin's father, members of the movement called the New Enlightenment, looked down on these simple people for their ignorance and superstition, but the ecstatic joy of their religion, their sense of oneness with God, man, and nature, were appealing to a child. Martin Buber was fascinated with them, and, though he was unaware of it at the time, his mind was storing up impressions that were to have a lasting influence on his life.

Martin would always remember the short, happy summers at Sadagora. There were almost twice as many daylight hours for play as during the winter at Lemberg, and his playground was vast. He raced through the fields and up and down the dusty lanes. The wind, rippling over the buckwheat and rye, blew teasingly against his face and through his hair. Sometimes he stopped to listen to the song of the lark high above his head, or to watch a group of peasants tossing pitchforks of hay into a cart, and he felt a part of all he saw and heard. The sky and the tender white clouds drifting across it seemed to draw close to him, and at night the friendly stars twinkled and blinked as if they were no farther away than the nearest treetop.

There was a horse in his grandfather's stable, a large dapple-gray that was Martin's delight. When the boy came near, the horse lifted his large head, flicked his ears, and gave a whinny of recognition. It seemed to Martin to be a signal saying he was approved. They were like fellow conspirators, sharing a secret no one else knew. Martin poured oats into the manger, and while the horse was eating, he talked gently to him as if he understood, while stroking the long mane, sometimes smooth and beautifully combed, and sometimes wildly tangled. He felt the quiver of life beneath his hand, and with it an exhilaration that seemed as though he had been drawn toward some deep, mysterious force, something that was neither the horse nor himself alone. "If I explain it now," he wrote long afterward, "I must say that what I experienced in touch with the animal was the Other, the immense and otherness of the Other which, however, did not remain strange like the otherness of the ox and ram, but rather let me draw near and touch it."

Once, in the summer of Martin's eleventh year, he felt a sudden awareness of his hand stroking the animal's mane and the vibrant skin beneath, and he thought of himself and his own sensation, apart from the Other. It was a small thing, but to the sensitive boy there was a change. The mysterious sense of oneness was broken. He went to the stable the next day and poured a heaping measure of oats for the horse and stroked him as usual while he ate, but something was missing. The horse had not lifted his head and given the whinny of welcome when he approached, nor did he seem to take any notice of the boy's stroking hand and softly spoken words. When Martin Buber had grown old and wise, he could look back on the incident and still remember the anxiety of a small boy imagining he had been judged and found wanting.

He was never to lose that sense of kinship with the life around him. As a man he would again and again refer to it, writing or telling of one who could put his arms around a young tree and feel the same surge of life as in himself, or who looked in the eyes of a dumb animal and read his own special mystery. "We experience the ripening and fading of far distant stars as something which happens to us, and there are moments when our organism is a wholly other piece of nature."

The wind grew sharper and colder as it blew in from the Russian plains. It moaned through the trees of the woodlot, sending down showers of yellow birch leaves. With the late summer rains the forest floor, clear of undergrowth and as neat as if swept by a housewife, became cluttered with ghostlike mushrooms. Birds gathered in flocks among the tree branches, chattering excitedly as they prepared for their migration. High overhead the wild swans flew southward, guided by the flutelike call of their leader. This was a busy time on the Buber estate, for there, too, preparations were being made to leave. Peasants wearing long white smocks moved through the grainfields, reaping, binding the sheaves, and carrying them to the threshing floor.

Adele Buber kept a close eye on the management of the estate. In long narrow ledgers she entered the expenses and income, and counted the profits or loss. Here and there among the accounts were quotations from great thinkers or something of her own, a motto or proverb, written in her strong, formal style of German.

The grain was sold, with enough left in the granary to feed the animals until the next year's harvest. The stables and barn and sheepfold were made secure for the hard winter. And for Martin there was one last good-bye to the sheep, the oxen, the noisy clamoring geese, and to the beloved dapple-gray, before the long ride back to their house in town. They returned in September, in time for the Jewish New Year, and that most sacred of days that came soon afterward, the Day of Atonement.

When Martin was thirteen he was given his first phylacteries, the two small leather cases men wore bound to the forehead and to the left arm for their weekday morning prayers. Inside the cases were small strips of parchment on which were written words from the holy laws of Moses:

"And these words which I command you this day shall be in your heart: And you shall teach them diligently to your children, and shall talk of them when you sit in your house, and when you walk by the way, and when you rise up. And you shall bind them for a sign upon your head and they shall be as frontlets between your eyes."

At thirteen, Martin Buber had come of age. He was old enough now to be responsible for his actions, for good or ill. In a former generation he would have been old enough to have a wife chosen for him. He was old

enough also to take part in the synagogue services, and
to be called up to read from the Torah. The prayers he
chanted were no longer the prayers of a child. He
looked down at the prayer shawl wrapped around him,
attentively regarding it as his grandfather's prayer book
instructed, "pressing the fringes with the devotion of the
eyes, and kissing them with fervor as a sign of attach-
ment to the law of which they are a memorial." He
prayed that as in this world he enveloped himself in the
material scarf, so might he become worthy to wear the
robe of wisdom, and the beautiful scarf of spiritual
purity in the world to come. As he prayed, the written
words inside the phylacteries he wore on his forehead
and on his left arm burned deep in his memory.

That year, for the first time, Martin fasted the full
twenty-four hours on the Day of Atonement, as the
adults did. On the day before, he had asked forgiveness
of his grandparents and his father for any mischievous
deeds he had done, and he forgave and was forgiven for
whatever boyish quarrels there had been between his
playmates and himself. Before the sun went down he
joined the family for the last meal until the next evening
after the first three stars appeared in the sky. He took
the piece of bread his grandfather blessed and passed to
him, dipped it in honey, and silently ate it with his soup.
The usual Sabbath songs and laughter were missing.
There was little talk at the table on this one day of the
year, but there were affection and tenderness felt by one
for the other without the need of words. To Martin
Buber the meaning of this day came with a force he had

not experienced before. He saw the sun slowly disappear and the slow fading of the clouds in the west, and then the holy day began.

That night he lay in his bed wide awake long after the other members of the family had gone to sleep. There were so many laws to remember on this day, now that he had become an adult, so many mystical directions from the prayer book of things forbidden and things he must do. He must not wash during the whole twenty-four hours unless it was to remove positive uncleanliness, though he might pour the ritual water over his fingers for the first prayer of the morning. He must not wear shoes of leather. He must remember the special prayers that were to be intoned on this day only.

The sound of footsteps passing outside his window died away, and only the ticking of the clock, with chimes that marked the hours, broke the silence of the night. At long last a faint shimmer of light came through the closed window. Masses of shadows began to take on their true shapes: the clay stove, the bureau, chair, washstand with bowl and pitcher. When these could be clearly seen from a distance of four feet, it was time to get up.

"And then, when the sleepless night was heavy upon me and very real, my body, reacting already to the fast, became as important to me as an animal marked for the sacrifice," Martin Buber wrote later, in describing it to a friend. "This is what formed me: the night, and the following morning, and the Day itself, with all its hours, not omitting a single moment."

The father must have felt some concern for this fervent young son, whose eyes, too serious for his years, seemed to be searching far into the unknown. He took Martin with him to one of the more liberal synagogues for the Day of Atonement morning service. The prayers took on a deeper meaning for Martin, now that, as a man, he could take part in the services. He enunciated the syllables distinctly, as the prayer book directed, and dwelt on each word so that it impressed itself like a white flame in his soul:

" 'Then shall all the inhabitants of the world know and acknowledge that unto Thee every knee shall bend.' " Here Martin bent his knee, to the amazement of the sophisticated worshipers around him. " 'Before Thee, O Eternal our God, shall we kneel and fall prostrate, and we shall ascribe honor to Thy glorious name.' " With these words he bowed his head and let it rest on his left arm, as an act of prostration. He sensed disapproval on all sides as eyes stared down at him, and on his father's face was a look of embarrassment and annoyance.

The next year, in 1892, Martin Buber left his grandparents' home and went to live with his father, who had remarried and was living at Lemberg. In that same year, when he was fourteen, he put away the phylacteries and the fringed prayer shawl, never to wear them again.

2 SCHOOL AND UNI-VERSITY YEARS

IN LEMBERG THERE WERE THREE CATHOLIC CATHEDRALS, ROMAN, GREEK, AND ARMENIAN. Like a symphony, the chime of their bells, mingling one with another, could be heard throughout the city. And on the Jewish New Year, called also the Day of Judgment, the air resounded with the blowing of the great ram's horn.

In the synagogue schools the boys Martin's age were ready to go from the Torah, which they should have learned thoroughly, to the books of explanation, the Talmud and the Midrash. But these books, one containing the sages' interpretation of the holy laws and the

35

other commenting on them in a poetic and philosophical way, were left out of Martin Buber's education, for
his father had had him enrolled in a secondary public
school.

Though the school was secular, open to all faiths, the
pupils were called upon every morning to recite together the Christian creed of belief in the Trinity. Martin, with the few other Jewish boys in the school, stood
during the recital with heads bowed, staring at the floor,
the words of their morning prayer still fresh in their
memory: *Hear, O Israel, the Lord our God, the Lord is
One*. The teachers showed no religious prejudice, and
made no effort to persuade them to join in, but to the
boys there was a greater loneliness in being ignored,
treated as if they were invisible, than if their religious
beliefs had been challenged.

During this time Martin with his inquiring mind
found many things to wonder about. The mysteries of
time and space puzzled him. Does time go on and on
and on, never coming to an end? The thought was ap-
palling. Or would time eventually reach an end, and
come to a stop? If so, what then? This was even more
frightening to anticipate. And what about space? Does
it stretch out, limitless, without boundary. Or is there
somewhere an edge to space? Had time and space a beginning? If so, what went before? Martin's thoughts
wavered from one terrifying possibility to the other, and
he could find no answer.

When he had been in the secular school a year, he
came across a book meant for the teachers, as it was too

A modern-day rabbi demonstrates the use of the shofar, *or ram's horn, still used to signal the approach of the Jewish New Year.* (CULVER PICTURES, INC.)

advanced for the average pupil. It was *Prolegomena to All Future Metaphysics,* by the German philosopher Immanuel Kant. In reading it he discovered that many learned men had puzzled over this same mystery that had been torturing him. Kant's argument was that time and space existed only in man's limited understanding. They were not part of the inner nature of the world. The mystery of time and space was the mystery of man's own being, of his own grasp of knowledge.

For four years Martin Buber led the life of the typical European schoolboy of his time. The masters were exacting and severe. So many hours had to be spent in study that there was little time for play and recreation, and no time at all for sports. Many a boy, hunched over his books in a cold, dreary schoolroom, must have dreamed of the glorious freedom he would have as a university student. In the meantime he had to endure the strict regime of constant drilling so he would be prepared. He parsed sentences and conjugated verbs. He translated Cicero into Polish; he memorized the dates of wars and reigns of kings; and he solved problems in algebra and geometry. For Martin, time seemed to stand still except for the short, carefree summers at Sadagora, but the day came at last when he took his final examination at the secondary school and was ready to enter the University of Vienna.

The life of a university student in Europe was a complete contrast to that of a schoolboy. A student's only obligation at the university was to register and to pay for a certain number of lectures. He could choose his own courses, as many as he wanted, and on whatever subjects interested him. He could attend the lectures or not, as he felt inclined; it would make no difference in his standing as a student. He could go from one university to another, changing at his will, and he could choose the professors he wanted to study under. The decision was his as to when and where he would receive his degree, but the degree would be given him only if he knew his subject well. It was not earned according to a certain number of points or hours of credit, but according to the knowledge a student acquired. And he would have to prove that knowledge by reading his thesis before a jury of brilliant men, specialists in the chosen subject, and argue its points with them.

Martin Buber bought a lecture schedule to decide upon his subjects. There were so many to choose from, and he wanted to explore them all. For his main subjects he chose philosophy, for which the University of Vienna was famous, and the history of art.

Lemberg had once seemed a bustling metropolis, with its pair of majestic stone lions, symbols of the city's name, its town-house tower rising high above the tree-tops, and the busy little Peltew flowing on its way to join the river Bug. Now, compared to the excitement of Vienna, it had shrunk to the size of any ordinary town. It was strange, after the medley of languages in Lemberg, to hear only German spoken in classrooms and halls, in coffee shops where students gathered, along the tree-lined Ringstrasse that led to the university. The way it was spoken in Vienna was especially beautiful,

Martin thought, so rich and vibrant. What a treasure lay waiting for one with a command of the language, who could fashion words and phrases to express the most elusive of thoughts!

He browsed among the sidewalk bookstalls, and found a choice of German books that would have been the delight of his grandmother in her youth. At the National Theatre, adjoining the palace grounds and a short walk from the university, he heard the language as the actors spoke it, pronounced in a way to give a word its slightest shade of meaning. Day after day he stood in line, sometimes for hours, to buy his ticket; then he rushed up three flights of stairs to the topmost balcony, where he listened, enthralled. Words he had known only in books came alive, moving, able to create every change of emotion. Buber was sure by then he would become a writer, a master of words.

The latest literary sensation of Austria at that time was Hugo von Hofmannsthal, a sensitive poet whose words fairly sang from the pages. Buber learned that he was twenty-two then, only four years his senior. He had been writing since he was a schoolboy, and his first publication was a poetic drama, written when he was sixteen. His poem "Song of Life" began: "Let the heir be a squanderer." Buber read the copy he had bought at a bookstall, enchanted. The melodious words seemed to pour forth with no effort. This lavish use of the language, buoyant, ecstatic, like treasures scattered by a spendthrift heir, delighted Martin Buber. This same style crept into his own first writings. Later, when his style became more disciplined, he learned that Hofmannsthal, whose words seemed to flow so easily, also struggled, desperately writing, discarding, beginning anew, and declaring that language was still inadequate to express man's thoughts and emotions.

After a year in Vienna, Buber went to the University of Berlin, where there was an overwhelming choice of lectures, and a faculty that included some of the country's most brilliant men. One, the well-loved Wilhelm Dilthey, then sixty-four, was considered one of Germany's greatest thinkers. Another, Georg Simmel, though twenty-five years younger, had made a reputation for himself throughout Europe and in America, and his teachings were influencing some of the philosophical thinking of the time.

There was a spirit of rebellion among the younger generation as the nineteenth century was drawing to its close. Artists revolted against the formal, academic style of their elders, and were trying new perspectives and designs, distorting when it was desirable, and painting in colors either pale and shimmering or wildly barbaric. During the year Martin was in Vienna, a group of artists, young bearded rebels, seceded from the conservative Academy and formed what they called a movement of *Sezession*. Poets were creating, in vowels and words, impressions of mood, color, and music. Musicians were shocking the traditionalists with new harmonies, discordant at times. In religion and philosophy old ideas and beliefs were being challenged, and great thinkers of the past who had been neglected or persecuted during their lifetime were being rediscovered and admired. Scientists were making undreamed-of strides, upsetting many of the old beliefs, and questions were being asked that were never asked before, for which there was often no answer.

In this atmosphere Martin Buber spent his student years. The German student, with his reputation for recklessness and gaiety, his jolly drinking songs, dances, love affairs, his duel scars proudly displayed, had also a serious side. In many a coffeehouse or beer garden students held long discussions about art, politics, philosophy, or religion.

They talked of Friedrich Nietzsche, over fifty years old then, and hopelessly insane, who was just becoming recognized for the work of his early years. He was especially popular with young people who found courage in his message that one should become master of life and not its slave. Man was free to do what he wanted with himself, he had written. He could, like the inferior man, lead a passive existence, with security, leisure, contentment his only goals. Or, like the superman, he could reach inward for the inexhaustible potentialities that lie dormant within every human being, waiting only to be awakened. "And this secret spake Life herself to me, 'Behold,' said she, 'I am that which ever must surpass itself.' "

The first of Nietzsche's books that Buber read was his *Thus Spake Zarathustra*. Here was a new kind of literature, he decided, a literature of ideas in which the individual point of view was stressed. Man was still in the

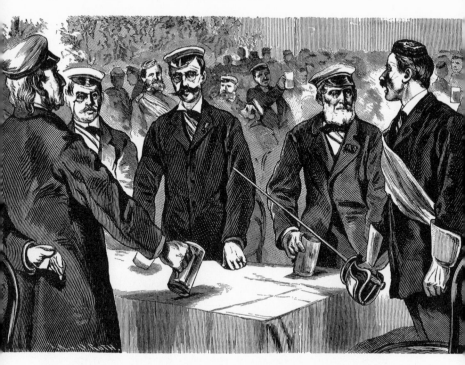

An engraving from the late nineteenth century shows German university students enjoying themselves. (CULVER PICTURES, INC.)

making, Nietzsche said. He was the only animal who could, through his own will to power, raise himself beyond his ordinary life.

A generation before Nietzsche, another philosopher, also unappreciated and neglected in his time, had said, "An existing individual is constantly in the process of becoming." Soren Kierkegaard had been dead for over forty years, but only then were his works being translated from Danish into German. The young intellectuals took up his ideas, giving him the recognition that had been denied him while he lived. Man exists and chooses, he had said. No one has his way planned for him. He must gather up the courage, in his loneliness and anguish, to make his own choice, with no way of knowing what the outcome will be.

The lecture rooms where the professors Dilthey and Simmel taught were always crowded. Both stressed the idea of the whole man, the relationship of mind and body and the connection of all that went on in the mind of man in relation to the past, and to the present world about him. Through the teachings of these men, and through the writings of the world's great thinkers, from Plato and Aristotle down to his own time, Martin Buber was taking his first steps toward developing a philosophy of his own, that of the unity of man with his Creator, and with all His creation. He was going through periods of rejecting, accepting, or developing further the thoughts of the great philosophers. He asked himself questions and searched for the answers.

"What is man?" Kant had asked, thinking in terms of man's capacity to think, to feel, to act. Buber carried his question beyond this. What is man's special place in the universe? he asked. What is man's connection with destiny, his relation to the world of things, his understanding of his fellowmen, his existence as a being that knows it must die, his attitude in all the ordinary and extraordinary encounters with the many and varied mysteries of life?

Buber's studies took him to the universities of Leipzig and of Zurich. He took courses in psychiatry so that he might know man in all his phases, pathological as well as normal. There was a revival of interest in mysticism then, and he became interested in the philosophy of the Orient and in the Christian mystics of the Renaissance. For his doctorate he studied the German Christian mystics. There were two who especially impressed him, and who had some influence on his own thought, Meister Eckhart and Jakob Boehme. Eckhart had meditated on time and eternity, and on the relation between God and human thought, six hundred years earlier. He considered the union of the human and the divine the highest goal of man. "I have need of God, but God has need of me!" he had declared. Sacraments, pilgrimages, fasting, penances were all meaningless unless man had the divine spark in his soul. Boehme, born in 1575, three hundred years after Meister Eckhart, stressed the same thought of the divine within the soul of man. It is ever present, he said, but man cannot become aware of it until he subdues his own selfish thoughts and desires, his concern with comfort and ambition:

"If you can, my son, for a while but cease from all your thinking of self and willing of self, then you shall hear the unspeakable words of God.

"My son, when you are quiet and silent, then you are as God was before nature and being. You are that which God was: you are that whereof He made your nature and being."

The young intellectuals of all faiths were rebelling against the narrow, unbending religion of their fathers. They took comfort in the teachings of the great men of the ages who had also rebelled. They quoted Nietzsche's startling words *God is dead,* that is, the God of his stern, bigoted upbringing. They also quoted Meister Eckhart, who had referred to God as *Nothing,* meaning not that God did not exist but that he had a more profound existence than any created being. Boehme had written of God as *Underneath,* rather than above. Nature rises out of God; we sink into Him. Nothing but good comes out from *Underneath,* though there may be good that endures or good that fails.

In 1901, while Martin Buber was working on his dissertation about the German mystics, he came across a treatise on the Lord's Supper written by a young professor of theology at the University of Strassburg, Albert Schweitzer. He was impressed by Schweitzer's understanding of the close relation of Jesus and the mysteries of Jewish faith. Schweitzer had been given the subject as a thesis while still a student, he learned, and had gone about preparing for it with the same thoroughness he put into everything he was ever to do. He had studied the Hebrew language for a better understanding of the Old Testament, and he had made a study of Hebrew customs and rituals of the time of Jesus. Here was a realistic theologian, Buber said. He found in this treatise an incentive for his own studies on the subject.

He began a thorough study of the New Testament, and discovered in Jesus' teachings the devout faith of Judaism: "Think not that I am come to destroy the law or prophets. I am come not to destroy, but to fulfill. . . . Therefore all things whatsoever ye would that men should do to you, do ye even so unto them: for this is the law and the prophets." The word *law,* in Buber's opinion, was a Greek mistranslation of the Hebrew word for the teachings of Moses. *Torah* meant direction, instruction, information, not law or commandments. Throughout the sayings of Jesus he found reference to these instructions that every Jew learns in his childhood. "Which is the first commandment of all?" a scribe asked. And Jesus replied with those sweet and holy words Jews all over the world have chanted day after day for forty centuries: "Hear, O Israel; the Lord our God is one Lord: And thou shalt love the Lord thy God with all thine heart, and with all thy soul, and with all thy might."

"I have found in Jesus my great brother," Buber has said. He knew Jesus from within as no Christian could know him, for he understood the stirrings and impulses of his Jewish being. Even in his last agony Jesus had spoken those haunting lines from the Psalms, "My God, my God, why hast thou forsaken me?"

Buber wrote: "I am more than ever certain that a great place belongs to him in Israel's history of faith, and that this place cannot be described by any of the usual categories."

Though Martin Buber had given up the rituals, no longer wore the phylacteries, ate the unleavened bread at Passover, or fasted on the Day of Atonement, the unbroken faith of his people was too much a part of him for him to think of changing. He saw many of the Jewish students turn away from Judaism. Some became converted to Christianity, some to atheism, and some substituted the teachings of Karl Marx for their religion.

"It is time's great heritage that we bring with us into the world," Buber said of Judaism. "We Jews need to know that our being and our character have been formed not solely by the nature of our fathers but also by their fate, and by their pain, their misery and their humiliation. We must feel this as well as know it, just as we feel and know within us dwell the elements of the prophets, the psalmists and the kings of Judah."

He felt not only a part of the past but also of the present. There came to his mind the poor of eastern Europe he had seen in his childhood, "the miserable, stooped people," he called them, "dragging their feet, peddling their wares from village to village, not knowing where their next day's livelihood was coming from, not even knowing why they should go on living." He described the great masses emigrating to escape hardship and persecution, being loaded aboard ship, not understanding where they were going or why. He suffered not merely for them; it was as though their troubles had been transferred to him. "My soul is not by the side of my people. My people *is* my soul," he said.

During the year he had been at the University of Vienna, he came across a pamphlet, newly published, by Theodor Herzl, called *The Jewish State*. It contained a message of hope and courage for scattered, uprooted Jews throughout the world, as well as a plan showing how they could form once again a nation of their own. If they could be granted sovereignty over a portion of the globe large enough to satisfy the requirements of a nation, they could manage the rest. There they could live at last as free men on their own soil, and peacefully in their own homes, Herzl had said.

In 1897 Buber attended the first Zionist Congress, in Basel, Switzerland. People were gathered there from every country in Europe, from America, from Asia Minor, from Egypt, to hear more of Herzl's message. They were as mixed a group as could be imagined. Among them were millionaires, world famous, and peddlers of secondhand clothes, professors, novelists, poor students who had hiked miles to attend, illiterate peasants sent by their community, and bearded Talmudic scholars with skullcaps and long side curls. They were united in one desire, to set forth on another exodus and re-create their lost nation. A proposal was made

Theodor Herzl (1860–1904), the Austrian journalist and founder of Zionism. (THE GRANGER COLLECTION)

that they should buy land and send pioneers to prepare the way. The question was where this land should be. Some considered a sparsely settled South American country; others thought of some colony in Africa. A cry went up among the people. They would build their nation only in Palestine, the land that had been promised them through Abraham, Jacob, and Moses.

In spite of the long centuries they had been separated as a people, their rituals and their prayers had remained unchanged. And every prayer or psalm they chanted, at home or in the synagogue, was filled with yearning to return to this holy land. Three times a day, for almost two thousand years, the prayer was sung: "Sound the great horn of our freedom, lift up the banners to gather us from the corners of the earth to our land." And every year at the Passover supper they said to one another, "Today we are here. Next year may we be in Jerusalem."

Palestine was then part of the Turkish Empire, and occupied by Arabs whose ancestors had also a claim on this land. One group of Zionists argued that they should use political means to carry out their plan. They should win the sympathy of the big powers, and apply to the Turkish government for a charter giving them permission to build their colony. They would then migrate in such vast numbers they would be safe against any aggression. Martin Buber was among those opposing this idea. It was better for a people to be prepared for the land than for the land to be prepared for the people, he argued. Instead of a sudden, poorly planned mass settlement, he wanted to see a thorough preparation, taking generations if necessary; for the rebirth of the Jewish nation should be spiritual as well as physical.

When he received his Ph.D. and his student days were behind him, he had more time to devote to the Zionist cause. He worked for a while as one of the editors of a Zionist publication called *The World*. As the split widened between the political and the cultural Zionists, Buber saw the policy of the magazine become more and more nationalistic. He resigned in protest. Israel, with her great heritage, could be something more than one small nation among many small nations, he believed. He wanted to see a reawakening of the intellectual and spiritual traditions. Then there were the Arabs to consider. It wasn't enough to try to win their confidence only to establish the new colony. There should be a genuine solidarity between Jews and Arabs, both working together and helping each other to a better way of life.

Chaim Weizmann, a brilliant young research chemist four years older than Buber, shared these views. The two men brought together a small group with the purpose of calling on Jews of all the German-speaking countries to work toward a rebirth of Jewish culture. They dreamed of another Renaissance, with a revival, after long neglect, of learning and art. Buber's former teacher, Wilhelm Dilthey, encouraged them and gave advice. He pointed out that the Italian Renaissance had been universal and not nationalistic, that it had been

Chaim Weizmann (1874–1952), the Russian-born chemist, who shared Buber's enthusiasm for the Zionist cause. (THE GRANGER COLLECTION)

concerned with man as an individual as well as with the community of men.

The group founded a publishing firm so they could introduce works on the cultural ideals of Zionism. Weizmann and Buber planned also to publish a magazine to be called simply *Jude*. After getting out a manifesto of their project, they had to abandon the idea. In that year, 1904, Chaim Weizmann was invited to England to lecture on biochemistry at the University at Manchester.

The realization came to Buber during this time that he knew very little about the cultural history of his people. "I professed Judaism before I really knew it," he said. He had missed the books that for so long had been the basis of every pious Jew's education, the Talmud and the Midrash, nor did he know the Kabbala and the Zohar, or Book of Splendor, the source of many of his grandmother's tales. He now turned to those books, and then to the ones that came after them. Some told of false messiahs who lived in princely splendor through preying on the superstitions of their followers, and some told of saintly men who gave hope to their people, encouraging them to cling to their faith in spite of hardship and persecution.

One day in his reading Buber came across a quotation from Israel ben Eliezer, known as the Baal Shem Tov, or Master of the Wonderful Name of God: "He arises in eagerness from his sleep, for he is sanctified and has become another man and is worthy to create, and imitates God by forming his world." These words, spoken some two hundred years earlier, impressed Buber as if they had been addressed directly to him. This description of the joy of daily renewal felt each morning upon awakening could apply to newly awakened nations as well as to man.

He remembered the Hasidim of Galicia, how fascinated he had been by the fervor of their worship. Once he had seen their leader striding with dignity among the rows of the faithful, and he had felt the power of the man. But all he knew about them was through his observations as a child, and he knew nothing at all of their history. He began research on the founding of the sect, and the early followers. The first masters taught mostly in parables, in a way that simple, uneducated villagers could understand, but in their teachings Buber discovered an astounding wisdom.

That year Martin Buber, then twenty-six, gave up his writing and publishing, and his work with the Zionists. For the next five years he lived in seclusion, to carry on his search into the beginnings of Hasidism.

3 STUDY OF THE HASIDIC LEGENDS

HASIDISM HAD ITS ORIGIN IN THE UKRAINE, ON THE COLD, RUGGED SLOPES OF THE CARPATHIANS, close to the Dniester River. It began as a religion of the poor and oppressed, but it soon spread to take in half the Jews in eastern Europe. In the eighteenth century the people, living under the constant threat of persecution, and disillusioned time and again by false messiahs, were ready for a religion that would lift them out of their despair. The long and tedious explanations of the Torah, which scholars pored over, were beyond their understanding, yet it was written in the Talmud that no ignorant man could be pious.

In the teachings of Hasidism they learned that knowledge was of less importance in forming the quality of man than the purity and devotion of his soul. God does not hold himself aloof from His creation, they were told. He is everywhere within it, in all man's words and thoughts and deeds, in animals and plants, in hills and valleys and in the stones that crop up from the earth.

"God is hidden in every secret place in the secret of secrets. Everything that lives, grows, rises and praises God in song. Every blade of grass sings a song to God," said one of the early masters.

There is nothing that is evil and unworthy of love, the Baal Shem Tov taught. Even the urges of man are not evil, for they can be turned to good as night turns into day. Each new day was a new beginning, and every second of it that passed was to be hallowed. The worshipers, poor and unlettered though they might be, and far from perfect, felt within themselves the presence of the Divine, and they sang and danced in the joy of their religion.

> Where I wander—You!
> Where I ponder—You!
> Only You, You again, always You!
> You! You! You!
>
> Sky is You! Earth is You!
> You above! You below!
> Only You, You again, always You!
> You! You! You!

There had been many changes since the early days of Hasidism. As the movement grew, it was split into separate communities, each with its own leader called a righteous one, or zaddik. This leadership was inherited by a son or disciple, instead of going to the one most worthy spiritually. Some of the leaders, unlike the first ones, lived in the ease and luxury of royalty, holding themselves aloof from the people who supported them. Unprincipled and ambitious men came forward, proclaiming themselves leaders also, drawing the superstitious to them through fraud and claims of magic. Rivalries developed among the communities, with bitter quarrels between one zaddik and another, causing a spiritual deterioration in the movement.

In his search Buber collected everything he could find that had been written about the beginning of Hasidism. In old books of the people, in chapbooks, sometimes even on stray scraps of paper, he found stories or sayings of a beloved master written by a disciple from memory or hearsay. He also went to Galicia where he could talk with the old men who could remember tales told to them in their youth. Legends had grown around the Baal Shem Tov and his first successors, as they will when a story is handed down through the spoken word from one generation to the other. The Hasidic legend, Buber found, had not the vigor of the Buddhist legend or the intimacy of the St. Francis of Assisi legend: "It did not grow up in the shade of ancient groves, nor on hills clad with silvery olive trees. In

narrow streets and gloomy little rooms, it passed in awk-
ward words to ears that listened in fear."

Buber pictured the little room where the master, gentle and wise, sat with his disciples, teaching them by
parable and allegory. There were true leaders at that
time, with the humility that goes with greatness. Not
only did they feel the presence of the Divine; they also
felt the spirit of others within themselves, and they felt
themselves in others. "In the beginning I wished of God
that I might suffer the pain and needs of Israel," said the
Baal Shem Tov's great-grandson. "But now, when one
person tells me of his pain, I feel the pain more than he
does, for he can forget it, and I cannot."

It was told of another leader that he once took in a
drunken peasant and made a bed for him in his home.
To those who disapproved he answered, "If God suffers
this man in His world, then it is where he belongs. So
must I, too, suffer him in my world." Again, when he
gave money to a scoundrel, he said to his disciples, "I
also am not good, yet God gives me what I need." Once
a rabbi watched in silence when thieves broke into the
adjoining room, and helped themselves to what they
wanted. One of the thieves picked up a water jug.
"Don't take that," the rabbi called out. "You can have
anything else you want, but a sick man drank from that
jug today, and his breath might still be on it to give the
disease to you." After that, every night before going
to bed the rabbi declared everything he owned to be
ownerless, so that if thieves broke in again, the burden
of sin would not be upon them.

The Baal Shem Tov left nothing of his own in writing, and he refused to allow anyone to write about him during his lifetime. One day, it was said, he saw a demon going through his house with a book in his hand. "What are you doing here? And what is that book you are carrying?" he demanded. "This is the book of which you are the author," the demon replied. The master knew then that someone was secretly writing down the things he said and did. He called his disciples together and wanted to know who was the guilty one. The disciple who had been taking the notes stepped forward with his written pages. The master looked them over, silently studying them page by page. "In all this there is not one word I have spoken," he said when he came to the end. "You were not listening for the sake of Heaven, and so the power of evil used you for its sheath, and your ears heard what I did not say."

Another time, when he was in the midst of a sermon, the Baal Shem Tov broke off suddenly in a fit of trembling. "O Lord of the world, you know that I am not speaking to increase my reputation," he exclaimed. There was a long pause; then the words came rushing from his lips: "Much I have learned and much I have been able to do, and there is no one to whom I can reveal it." And he said nothing more.

Though it was forbidden to write about him, tongues could not be silenced. The disciples talked among themselves of their master's greatness, of miracles he had performed, how he had healed the sick, raised the dead, driven out evil spirits, walked upon the waters of the Dniester River. The prophet Elijah had come down upon the earth with the announcement to the aged Rabbi Eliezer and his wife, Sarah, that God would bless them with a son, to be called Israel. The prophet Ahija the Shilonite watched over the child from his birth and taught him the ways of wisdom. When he grew to manhood, God spoke to him, bidding him to rise up and lead his people, and from time to time Abraham, Moses, and Elijah communed with him.

The legends grew with each telling. It was said that once the Baal Shem Tov was walking on a mountaintop so deep in meditation he failed to notice he was at the edge of an abyss. When he lifted his foot to step forward, the neighboring mountain immediately leaped over and pressed itself close to the spot, and the master walked calmly on. His son told of seeing him some time after his death in the shape of a fiery mountain bursting into countless sparks. "Why do you appear in such a shape?" the son asked. "Because in this shape I served God," was the reply.

These were recollections of pious men who, in the fervor of their devotion, spoke the truth as they believed it to be, and the things they told of were accepted as the truth because it was what the people desperately wished it to be. The stories, written in Yiddish, were often crude, filled with boring details or too sketchy, with important facts left out or distorted. But throughout them all was a conviction of a living relation with God. From the miracle-working and magic, charms and amulets, mountains that moved and pillars of fire that hovered over the pious, there also emerged the strong personality of a man, poor and uneducated, whose influence would be felt for a long time, and extend over a vast region. Some of the teachings of the Baal Shem Tov could be compared with those of the German mystics with whom Buber was familiar. Like Jakob Boehme he considered man as a whole being, one in mind, body, and soul, one with God, and one with all God's creation. And he believed, as did Meister Eckhart, that fastings, penances, pilgrimages had no meaning without the spirit of the Divine in one's soul. "Whoever mortifies his flesh will have to render account as a sinner," the Baal Shem Tov had said.

Israel, son of Eliezer, was late in acquiring his name Baal Shem Tov, Master of the Wonderful Name of God. Born in 1700 in the part of Galicia that was the Ukraine, of aged parents, he was left an orphan at an early age. The elders of the community, as was their custom, looked after him and saw that he was clothed and fed and had the same opportunity for an education the other children had. In the small, dismal room where the pupils sat swaying and chanting after their teacher, there was perhaps not one who showed less promise of spiritual leadership than the child Israel. Time after time, when he could no longer endure the airless room, he escaped and ran off to the mountain wilderness, only to be caught and brought back. The elders finally gave up, knowing they could do nothing with him, and left him alone.

He grew up alone, more at home in woods and fields

than in the village. There he learned the names of all the plants and came to know which ones had healing powers, and he pieced out an existence by digging the hillsides for clay, which he sold to the village potters. He was not lonely in his solitude, for he felt God's presence there. When he prayed or intoned the Psalms he remembered, it was with such intense rapture that the blood rushed to his head and his eyes glistened like sparks of fire. His body swayed, not in the slow, rhythmic way of men in a synagogue, but with such fervor that he trembled from head to foot in the sheer joy of communing with God. In his later years it was said of him that when he prayed, water in a trough trembled and swayed until he had finished, and grain in the barrels joined in the trembling. Even the fringes of his prayer shawl moved as if they had a body and soul of their own.

Israel ben Eliezer's fame began first as a healer, with his knowledge of herbs, and with charms and prayer. Later the word spread that he was wise in the way of settling disputes. The sick came to him, and those who wanted advice or judgment, and they stayed and listened to his words. He told them to be joyous, for the Divine Presence could not be felt through gloom and melancholy. They were not to be ashamed of their concern with everyday matters of living, he said. God was there too, and these things were made holy because of His Presence.

Those who had heard him and had witnessed his judgments and cures spread the news about his wisdom and sanctity, and people came from miles away. They gave him his name, the Baal Shem Tov, for surely, they said, he must have knowledge of the secret name of God to perform these miracles. A group of disciples gathered about him, praying as he prayed, in an ecstasy of song and dance. They chanted the Psalms with arms waving, hands clapping, with bows and jumps and little cries of joy. But joy in itself must not be their goal, the master told them. Their personal joy would come to them when they wanted nothing but the joy of God.

At the end of the day, after the evening prayer had been chanted, the disciples went to the master's room for instruction. The Baal Shem Tov sat before a table on which were two lighted candles and the mystic Book of Creation. When he spoke it seemed to each disciple that the words were directed intimately to him alone. On the day of Creation, the master said, God scattered the sparks of His Divine Being over all the earth. Thus He was everywhere, in all that He created. Man had it in his power, through dedicated devotion, to bring about a reunion of these sparks with the Creator.

"Alas," said the Baal Shem Tov, "the world is full of enormous lights and mysteries, and man shuts them from himself, as with a hand before his eyes, he shuts from view the greatest mountain."

"You ask about the holy Baal Shem Tov," said a disciple long after the master's death. "I tell you: if he had lived in the age of the prophets, he would have been a prophet. If he had lived in the age of patriarchs, he would have been great among them, so that as one says

'God of Abraham, Isaac, and Jacob,' it would also be said, 'God of Israel son of Eliezer.' "

It was two years after Buber became interested in Hasidism before his first book on the subject appeared. The work of collecting and assorting the material was tremendous. It meant a search for missing links, knowing what to discard and what to keep, learning to distinguish the authentic writings of those who had heard the teachings of the master, from additions made by later generations.

The first book was not about the Baal Shem Tov, but about his great-grandson Rabbi Nachman, whom Buber called the last of the great Jewish mystics. The degeneration of the movement had already begun in Rabbi Nachman's time, and he spent his life trying to bring about a return of the zaddik in the true meaning of the word: righteous, saintly, and a mediator between man and God.

Rabbi Nachman also put nothing down in writing. Unlike his great-grandfather, he did not forbid others to write about him, though he did not encourage it. His faithful disciple Nathan kept a record of everything he said. Immediately after the master had spoken, Nathan repeated what he had heard twice to others before writing it down so he would be sure to remember the exact words. Even at that his notes were confused, with additions and interpretations made by those who came later.

Rabbi Nachman could be compared to St. Francis of Assisi in the kinship he felt for all things living. "When man becomes worthy to hear the song of plants, how each plant sings its song to God, how beautiful and sweet it is to hear their singing!" he said. "Therefore it is good indeed to serve God in their midst in solitary wandering over the fields between growing things, and to pour out one's speech before God in truthfulness. All the speech of the fields enters into your own and intensifies its strength. With every breath you drink in the air of paradise, and when you return home the world is renewed in your eyes."

Once, it was said, he slept in a house that was built of slender young saplings, and he dreamed that he was lying among the dead. He reproached the owner of the house the next morning, saying that when one cuts down a tree before its time, it is as if one has murdered a soul.

Before Rabbi Nachman began his teaching, he had to satisfy the deep yearning he shared with every pious Jew of his time, to set foot on the holy soil of his ancestors. He was twenty-six when he started on the long, tiring journey from Galicia to Jerusalem. "The greater part of me is already there," he said to those who tried to discourage him. He had very little money, and had to leave his wife and children in the care of others. He knew that he would meet with obstacles at every stage of the journey, but he declared, "As long as there is breath in me, I will risk my soul, and go."

He was accompanied by the disciple Nathan, who kept a record of the pilgrimage. It was a record of hardships that would have turned back many a man with less determination, but to Rabbi Nachman there was no obstacle one could not overcome. In reality, he said, there were no obstacles except in the spirit.

All that he had known before journeying to the land of Israel was nothing, he said upon his return to Galicia. He settled in the town of Bratzlav to begin his teaching of Hasidism. The fame and riches of other zaddiks at that time might have been his also, but he chose to live among the people, sharing their poverty and their suffering. Sometimes his teachings were in the form of a fable or a fantasy of the kind the Grimm brothers were then collecting in Germany. Again his message would be short and simply told. "One must perfect himself so that he is wholly one, entirely good, thoroughly holy, as before creation," he said. "No limits are set to the ascent of man, to each the highest stands open. Here your choice alone decides," he said. Rabbi Nachman, like his great-grandfather, encouraged his followers to be joyous in their religion. Through joy the spirit is established, he told them. Through melancholy it goes into exile.

When he spoke, he wanted to feel a complete dialogue between his listeners and himself. He described this dialogue as a simple light that arises when one speaks to another, and a returning light. Sometimes it might happen that there is no returning light, but let the listener repeat the words he heard to someone else, and they will come back to him, impressing themselves in his mind. "When I begin to talk to someone, I want to hear the highest words from *him*."

Other zaddiks resented him because his humility and

piety were a reproach to their own way of life, and they made him an object of malicious slander. Rabbi Nachman was untouched by their persecution. Their words were like stones hurled against him that he would use to build with, he told his followers. It was at the time of the Napoleonic wars when he said, "The whole world is filled with strife, every country and every city and every house. When one realizes that man dies a little every day, for every day he must deliver to death a piece of himself, how then can he still be able to pass his days in strife?"

The *Tales of Rabbi Nachman* was followed by *The Legend of the Baal Shem* a year later, in 1907. These were not biographies in the ordinary sense of the word, Buber wrote. They did not rely on dates or facts or customs of the times. The lives of these two pious men were built out of the legends surrounding them, legends that showed the relationship between God and the universe as they had conceived it.

"The legend is the myth of *I and thou,* the inspired and the inspirer; the finite who enters the infinite," Buber stated in the preface of the second book. "The legend of the Baal Shem is not the history of a man, but the history of an inspiration. It does not relate his fortunes, but only his destiny. It does not move in a sequence of time, but in three cycles of consecration. Their end is already to be found in their beginning and in their end is a new beginning."

4 EARLY YEARS OF MARRIED LIFE

BEFORE HE BEGAN HIS STUDY OF THE HASIDIC LEGENDS, MARTIN BUBER TOOK AN EVEN MORE important step in his life by marrying Paula Winkler, whom he had known since his student years. She had warmth and imagination, and was as vivacious as he was quiet and studious. Theirs was a marriage of complete understanding, of companionship and shared interests, and a love that would last throughout their lives.

Tyrol, the mountainous region of western Austria that had been home to Paula, has been called a land of spirits. The jagged white peaks of the Alps rise ghostlike above the mist like floating mountains. When the mist

71

lifts, dark, mysterious forests appear as if newly created. Sometimes the wind comes howling in, and
streams dash in thundering torrents down the ravines.
At other times the wind is no more than a gentle mur-
mur, and calm lakes reflect a world turned upside down.
Here, it might be believed, the souls of the dead returned to wander the earth once more.

The carnivals of Tyrol were reminders of old beliefs,
when gods, now long forgotten, were worshiped, when
mountain fairies, meadow imps, and ice manikins were
as real as trees and mossy stones, when witches danced
away the winter snows, and evil spirits were propitiated
so no harm would come to the new spring grass. Paula
Buber's mind held a rich store of supernatural tales remembered from her childhood. Some of these she put
into books, which were written under the name of
Georg Munk.

There were memories of holy days also, the sweet
sound of bells calling the people to mass, the feel of
rosary beads between the fingers and a whispered
prayer with each one. *Hail, Mary, full of grace.* Christ-
mas carols on a snowy evening. Confirmation, a white
dress and veil and thoughts of Nazareth and Bethlehem.
The bishop had anointed her forehead, made the sign of
the cross, and placed his hand on her head, a symbol of
the Holy Spirit above her. Then she was given a light
rap on the cheek, a reminder that she must be ready to
suffer persecution for the faith.

At village inns in Tyrol, and in nearby Bavaria, also
familiar to Paula in her childhood, the villagers put on

plays. Some were plays so old their origin was un-known, and some were Passion plays, given at certain times in fulfillment of a vow made long ago. The Alpine village streets became, in the imagination, streets of Capernaum, Bethlehem, or Jerusalem. And for the moment the village wood-carvers, weavers, cobblers, bakers were scribes and publicans and fishermen on the Sea of Galilee.

Reminders of Zion appeared on every winding road, in wayside shrines with images carved in wood of the Madonna or Christ on a lonely cross. And in the churches each of the fourteen Stations of the Cross pointed the way to Calvary. *Lamb of God Who takest away the sins of the world, have mercy on us.*

Paula Buber gave up the religion of her people when she married and became converted to her husband's faith. She followed his interests in Zionism and in the mysticism of the Hasidic sect. Long afterward, when they were living in Jerusalem, Martin Buber wrote a poem recalling those early days of shared dreams and enthusiasms, which he presented to her in the latest of his many books on Hasidism:

> Do you still know, how we in our young years
> Traveled together on this sea?
> Visions came, great and wonderful,
> We beheld them together, you and I.
> How image joined itself with images in our hearts!
> How a mutual animated describing
> Arose out of it, and lived between you and me!
> We were there, and yet wholly here
> And wholly together, roaming and grounded.

Thus the voice awoke that since then proclaims
And witnesses to old majesty as new,
True to itself and you and to both together.
Take then this witness in your hands,
It is an end and yet has no end,
For something eternal listens to it and listens to us,
How we resound out of it, I and Thou.

Two children, Rafael and Eva, were born of this marriage, and they inherited the riches of both cultures. Buber wrote often about the miracle of birth and life's constant renewal: "In every hour the human race begins." Every hour that which was not became that which is, ten thousand beings which had never been seen before, each one unique and not like any other, ten thousand souls not yet developed, but ready to develop. "A creative event if ever there was one," he said. "Newness rising up in primal potential might."

He observed the development of all children through his own, the way they are constantly groping for knowledge, constantly learning. A child may willfully tear a sheet of paper; then he becomes absorbed in the shape it takes, and tries to make another like it. He is fascinated by the flicker of lamplight or the dance of leaves in a summer breeze, and reaches out in curiosity. Buber saw the close relationship that exists between the child and its mother, one that has no need for words. A child lying in his crib at bedtime sees the dark, lonely night gathering outside his window, slowly creeping into the room, and he listens for the sound of his mother's voice to know that he is safe. With some children, Buber said,

there was no need for the mother to speak. In the communion between mother and child there was a silent
dialogue that never breaks off, and the darkness holds
no terrors.

"A child is educated by the elements," he said in a
lecture, "by air and light and the life of plants and animals and he is educated by relationships."

The Bubers were living in Linz on the Danube, a
hundred miles west of Vienna, when the children were
small. Somewhere on the narrow picturesque streets of
town they might have passed a pale, slightly built youth
just out of secondary school. If so, they would scarcely
have given him a second glance, for there was nothing
about Adolf Hitler that would have attracted anyone's attention at that time. In school his grades had
been so poor that he failed to receive the customary cer-
tificate. He thought of himself as an artist, though his
talent was mediocre, and he was allowing his mother to
support him from her small pension.

Buber was working on a variety of subjects then. He
published a book of Celtic sayings, and he made a new
translation of *Kalevala,* the national epic poem of Fin-
land, keeping to the original meter. It was this meter
that had fascinated Longfellow, who used it in *The
Song of Hiawatha.* Oriental culture had been popular
for several years in Europe. The uncluttered style of
Chinese scroll paintings and Japanese prints were having an influence on European art. Tunes from Gilbert
and Sullivan's *The Mikado* were still being sung, and
Puccini's *Madama Butterfly* was produced in 1904.

Books on Oriental philosophy were translated into various languages. Buber translated from French into German a collection of Chinese ghost and love stories. Later he translated a selection of *Talks and Parables of Chuang-tzu,* who had carried on the teachings of Lao-tzu on the unity of man with the universe, when man has perfected himself. "Heaven and earth and I came together in existence, and I and all things are one."

Little is known about the Chinese sage Lao-tzu. He was probably born in the seventh century B.C. But where he lived and where he was buried still remain a mystery. In his sayings, called Tao, or the Way, there is much of the philosophy of the early masters of Hasidism, a striving toward perfection, a oneness with all things, returning good for evil. "Good men, I treat them well. Men who are not good, I also treat well. Virtue is good," said Lao-tzu. "True men, I deal with them truly. Men who are not true, I also deal with them truly. Virtue is true."

Chuang-tzu, born two and a half centuries later, rediscovered these sayings of Lao-tzu, which had been neglected all these years, and made them popular with the people. It was a time when China was split up into several feudal states, all owing allegiance to a weak ruler, and the people had become more and more regimented. But the perfected man, one who had attained unity through Tao, rose above government and society, according to Chuang-tzu. Things would work out all right if left to themselves.

In 1909, when Buber's translation of Chuang-tzu's

teachings was published, the twentieth century seemed still to be living up to its name, "The Century of Progress." Railways were expanding over all Europe. Electric lights and telephones were coming into the homes of ordinary people. Medical skills were constantly being improved, and sanitation took on a new importance. Automobiles were beginning to appear on cobbled village streets as well as in the cities. Marconi was working on a wireless system of communication, and the airplane had become something more than a fantastic dream.

In political affairs, however, the nations of the world were still bogged down in the past. The growth of industry had brought a spirit of strong competition among the different countries, which resulted in aggressive nationalism. Each tried to surpass the other in the size of armed forces. Britain, triumphant after the Boer War, the Boxer Rebellion, and skirmishes in India, ruled an empire that spread around the world, with the boast that the sun never set on the British flag. Francis Joseph still clung tenaciously to what was left of his once great Austrian Empire. France and Holland reached out for colonies as far as Southeast Asia. Almost the whole of Africa, from north to south, had been split up into colonies ruled by European powers. Even Spain, weakened by the loss of Cuba and the Philippines, held on to her African possessions.

Germany and Russia, newcomers to the Big Powers, were feeling their strength, and began to make up for lost time. Russia had turned to the East, but after having been defeated by small, emerging Japan, now faced the West. And Germany, victorious in her war against France, with Alsace and Lorraine added to her empire, looked about for more territory to conquer. The militarists had already twisted Nietzsche's "Will to Power" to justify aggression. "We must have a place in the sun!" was the cry.

In every country there were thinking men, few at first but their numbers growing, who looked beneath the surface and protested against what they saw. Behind the industrial prosperity was the squalor of slums, breeding places for disease, crime, frustration. The people were burdened with higher taxes, and the money was spent, not for social reforms, but for military preparedness. Secret alliances were suspected, and there existed a state of peace so fragile it could topple over like a house of cards, without warning. "We are papering over the cracks," Chancellor Bismarck had said a generation before, and it still held true.

The question was how to stop this headlong plunge to destruction. Some were for overthrowing existing governments by any means whatever to accomplish their ends. Others wanted to build on a more solid foundation a society free from exploitation by industrialism and irresponsible leaders. Since Bismarck's retirement in 1890, the Socialist government in Germany had been gaining strength. By 1912 it could claim over four million votes, with 110 members in the Reichstag, working with instead of against the existing government for reforms.

Mohandas Gandhi, then a lawyer in South Africa, was attracting attention by his passive fight for India's freedom and civil rights through nonviolence, or *Satyagraha,* which means "Force that is born of truth and love."

In 1913 Martin Buber read of one who had chosen another way of helping his fellowmen. Albert Schweitzer, whose treatise on the Mystery of the Last Supper had interested Buber twelve years earlier, had left Europe for the remote jungles of equatorial Africa as a medical missionary. He had spent the past eight years studying medicine, after having made a name for himself as a theologian, a philosopher, and a musician, in order to prepare himself for this work. Buber had called him a realist as a theologian when he first read the treatise. Now he called him a realist of the spirit as well, one who understood that man is not divided into two parts, a body and a soul. The true doctor, Buber said, treats man as a whole. Since physical suffering is more immediate, he treats that first, but he considers the soul at the same time. "If one approaches a doctor such as this," he wrote, "a man who is to begin with a theologian and who is destined to remain a theologian as long as he lives, and asks, 'Must you not first of all concern yourself with the soul?' he answers, 'The soul knows better how to wait than the body.' And in saying this he remained, in fact, in the following of his master who certainly did not begin again and again with the healing of bodily infirmities merely in order to give a sign."

Martin Buber might also have been called a realist of the spirit. When he read an article by Gandhi stating that the problems brought on by the industrial age could be solved only by going back to the simple ways of the past, he objected. "There is no such thing as Western civilization," Gandhi had written. "There is just modern civilization, which is a purely materialistic one. It, not England, governs India. If the British rule were replaced by an industrial Indian rule, the country would be no better off. East and West can only meet when the West has abandoned modern civilization."

Though Buber sympathized with Gandhi in his plea for individual rights and for a nation's right to govern itself, the thought of trying to hold back modern civilization was unrealistic. The West could not give it up, and the East could not avoid it. The spinning wheel would never take the place of textile mills. The flaming sword of the Cherubim barred the way back to the Garden of Eden, he said, but it also lighted the way forward.

A close friend of Buber's at that time, one who shared his views and perhaps had some influence on them, was Gustave Landauer, nine years his senior. They worked together on a modern translation of Meister Eckhart, but it was a common interest in social justice that brought them together.

"Everything that Landauer thought and planned and wrote, even when it had Shakespeare for a subject, or German mysticism, and especially all designs whatever for the building of a socialistic reality, was steeped in a great belief in revolution, and the will for it," Buber wrote of him.

Like Nietzsche, Landauer had asked: "Do we want to retreat into happiness? Do we want our lives for ourselves? Do we not rather want to do everything possible for the people, and long for the impossible? Do we not want the whole thing—Revolution!"

By Revolution he meant regeneration, a revolutionary conservation, one that would conserve all values worth keeping. He thought of Walt Whitman, whom he admired and whose poems he had translated, as an example of a conservative and a revolutionary spirit combined.

Between Landauer and Buber there was true dialogue. Whether in conversation or in silence, or at times when they disagreed, each had the other in mind, with no thought of what effect his own words or actions was having on the other.

In the spring of 1914, at Eastertime, a group of representatives from various European countries, alarmed at the feverish preparations for war, held a meeting in Potsdam. Buber and Landauer attended. There had been no agreement beforehand as to how the meeting would be conducted, yet from the first hour there was a bond of unity, each feeling a sense of identity with the others, though many were meeting for the first time. For three days they discussed ways of avoiding the catastrophe threatening the world, and how a closer understanding and unity among nations could be brought about. This preliminary meeting was so successful that plans were made for another meeting on a much larger scale in the following August.

Exactly two months later a revolver shot rang out in the town of Sarajevo, in Austrian-held Bosnia. Archduke Francis Ferdinand, heir to the Austrian throne, and his wife were assassinated by a Serb terrorist. A shudder of dread passed over the people of the earth. By August war had spread over the whole of Europe, from Russia to the British Isles.

The twenty-five-year-old Adolf Hitler, who had drifted from Linz to Vienna, living in municipal lodgings and earning a precarious livelihood painting postcards and advertisements, came to Munich. He had been rejected as unfit for military service in Austria, so he volunteered to serve in the German Army, where he was accepted. After poverty, uncertainty, and failures, he felt a sense of importance in uniform. When he was made a corporal, he experienced his first taste of authority over men below him.

With the beginning of the war, Martin Buber saw the abysses between man and man ever widening. Direct, frank dialogue, especially between men of different beliefs and different nationalities, was growing almost impossible. The Bubers had left Linz and were living in Berlin, where their many friends, some among the professors of the university, enjoyed the hospitality of their home. Buber, then thirty-six, set aside a certain time of the day for the students who wanted to come to question him and learn from him as he had, in his youth, visited his professors. Some were shy, perhaps, and a little in awe of the older, wiser man, but Paula, serving them coffee and cake, had a way of putting them at ease. A few of these students were afterward to become well known, among them Franz Kafka and Max Brod.

There was another period of the day when Martin Buber sat alone in his study, in quiet meditation. By erasing the things of the world from the mind and from the senses, one enters a state of nonbeing, and presses on to the Divine, so the mystics believe. To Buber, lifted out of the world of ordinary affairs, time lost its meaning. Past, present, and future were united, and all ages became one. The world's great thinkers, Lao-tzu, Plato, Meister Eckhart, Nietzsche, all were together in his thoughts. The voices of his family or the servants, the outside sounds of footsteps and the rattling of wheels, the ticking of the clock, the rustle of leaves against the windowpane, all faded from his ears as familiar sounds do that are heard but not listened to. His mind heard only words of wisdom uttered long ago.

One morning, after such a period of meditation, he came out to greet a young visitor, one who was a stranger to him. He was cordial to the youth, and tried to make him feel at home, but he was not with his visitor in spirit. He listened attentively, answered questions, and gave his opinion on philosophical matters that were brought up. But, he was later to learn, there were questions not asked, and never answered.

This happened a month or so after the war started. A short while later Buber learned that the young man had gone off to war and had been killed in battle. He was told also that the visit had not been a casual one. The youth had come in desperation, not for discussions, but for a decision. Buber felt that if he had been with his visitor in spirit as he had been in person, he would have guessed at the unasked questions and given his answers.

After that, there were no more periods of meditation for him. No longer would he seek to separate himself from the world about him. He rejected the Taoist idea of unity that is attained by rising above the material world, into an exalted state. This unity did not take in the whole man, in his entire existence, with his everyday life of hardship and sickness as well as his joys and sat-isfactions. It is not a true unity that can detach itself by turning away from the world. The great dialogue be-tween I and Thou was silenced. "The perfected man performs the non-action. He does not interfere in the life of beings, he does not impose himself upon them," said Chuang-tzu. But Buber said, "I am enormously con-cerned with just this world, this painful and precious fulness of all that I see, hear, taste, I cannot wish away any of its reality. . . . And how can I give this reality to my world except by seeing the seen with all the strength of my life, hearing the heard with all the strength of my life, tasting the tasted with all the strength of my life?" These sudden conversions, which Buber would experi-ence often in his life, he spoke of as "turnings."

The war dragged on from year to bitter year. Every-thing pointed to a German victory at first, owing to the years of military preparation. As time passed, the reports of glorious successes were fewer, and there were hints of losses, the seriousness of which could only be guessed. The people at home did not have to be told about the blockade. They felt it in shortages of food and fuel. Young boys who should have been behind desks in a schoolroom were being recruited and marched off, dressed in gray uniforms, goose-stepping, with left arms swinging, to kill or to be killed.

Thoughts of battle came pouring upon Martin Buber: "shrapnel wounds and tetanus, screams and death rattle, and the smile of the mouth above the crushed body." Where will this be bound in the heritage of the ages? he asked. "Where dwells its atonement, where sleeps its song, where does the secret of the master conceal itself?"

Buber and his family had left Berlin and were living in Munich. The German people had grown war-weary, and peace negotiations were called for. France and England considered the offer empty and insincere, declaring that they would settle for nothing less than restorations, reparations, and indemnities. The fighting continued. The winter of 1916 was the coldest in memory, with fuel at a premium and food so scarce that the time would long be spoken of as "turnip winter." There were demonstrations in the streets of Berlin, and protest marches denouncing the imperialist war. The leaders of the demonstrations were sentenced to prison, but this did not stop the bitter rumblings throughout the country.

In April 1917 the United States declared war on Germany. The Russian Army and Navy had revolted the month before, and the czar was forced to abdicate. By July the Socialist leader Kerenski was made prime minister. He had served only four months when the exiled Lenin returned to Moscow with the help of the Germans. He and Trotsky rallied the Bolsheviks around them and took over control of Russia. A series of political assassinations followed, beginning with the czar and every member of his family.

The Turkish Empire was near collapse. Mesopotamia, with Bagdad, the ancient capital of the Mohammedan world, fell to the British. Gaza followed, then Jaffa; and by the end of 1917 Jerusalem, too, was in the hands of the British.

Chaim Weizmann, who had worked with Buber in the Zionist movement, was still in England, engaged in important war work as a chemist in the Admiralty laboratories. This brought him in contact with important public figures, including Foreign Secretary Balfour, then first lord of the Admiralty. Through Weizmann's influence Lord Balfour wrote his famous letter to Lord Rothschild, promising a national home in Palestine for the Jews:

"His majesty's government view with favor the establishment in Palestine of a national home for the Jewish people, and will use their best endeavors to facilitate the achievement of this object, it being clearly understood that nothing shall be done that will prejudice the civil and religious rights of existing non-Jewish communities in Palestine, or the rights and political status enjoyed by Jews in any other country."

The following July, before the last of the Turks had been driven from Jerusalem and while fighting was still going on in Galilee, ceremonies were held in Jerusalem for the laying of the foundation stone of a Hebrew University. Chaim Weizmann sailed from London to give the address. Martin Buber had already renewed his interest in Zionism, and had launched a magazine of his own on the subject. Now he saw the beginning of the realization of the Jewish dream. There was so much to be done to rebuild the nation, practical things, such as roads and harbors, or simple needs, such as plows and shovels, yet it was typical that the first thought for the new country was a seat of learning. Men of vision saw this university of the future standing proudly on Mount Scopus. It would have the usual studies of a modern university: chemistry, bacteriology, geology, the humanities. But it would be different. Archaeological research, which in Egypt and Greece had discovered so many secrets of the past, was as yet untouched in Palestine. And from out of the past ancient Jewish learning would be linked with the present. Buber read the words of his friend's speech, and agreed.

"It is true that great social and political problems still face us and demand their solution from us," Weizmann had said. "We Jews know that when the mind is given fullest play, when we have a center for Jewish consciousness, then coincidentally we shall attain our material needs."

5 FRANZ ROSENZWEIG: A DIALOGUE BEGINS

ON THE NINTH OF NO-VEMBER THE GERMAN PEOPLE LEARNED THAT THEY had lost the war, that their Kaiser had abdicated and had flown to Holland for refuge, and that their allies, Austria-Hungary, Turkey, and Bulgaria, had surrendered a month earlier. On the eleventh an armistice was signed, with the demand of immediate evacuation of all German troops from Belgium, France, Alsace and Lorraine and the left bank of the Rhine. Six battle cruisers, ten battleships, eight light cruisers, fifty destroyers, and all submarines were to be interned at a place to be decided upon by the victorious nations.

Now that it was over, Martin Buber looked back on

the four years of savage fighting, and realized how deeply he had been affected by an evil he had been powerless to resist. Instead he had been compelled to live it, feeling within him the needless wounds, the pain, the suffering. "Oh, I have been terribly influenced!" he exclaimed. He turned his attention to ways of preventing war from ever happening again. He and his friends had many discussions on the subject.

Soldiers lucky enough to have survived came straggling home from the west and from the east, to find the whole country in a state of turmoil. The minor rulers of the German Empire, the King of Bavaria, who had reigned in Munich, and the kings of Saxony and Württemberg, had abdicated with the Kaiser, and different parties, both left and right, were fighting for control of the government. Some demanded Communism, as in Russia; some favored a more moderate form of Socialism. A few quiet voices might have spoken up for a democracy, as in the United States, or a constitutional monarchy, as in England and the Scandinavian countries, but no one would listen. The soldiers, leaderless now, refused to leave the army for the insecurity of civilian life. They joined the workers and formed a congress in imitation of the Russian Soviets. Sailors also mutinied and pushed for a revolution.

A once-proud nation, whose cities had been the best governed in the world, and whose schools and colleges had been models for other countries, was now reduced to a jungle of riots and arson and mass demonstrations. Money had become worthless, and life itself uncertain.

In Munich a Bavarian republic was proclaimed, independent of Prussia. Two months later the leader of this movement was murdered. Revolutions and antirevolutions, street fights and assassinations followed, and a change of government with each one.

Corporal Hitler, who had been injured in a gas attack and who was in a hospital when the armistice was signed, made his way back to Munich, still wearing his gray uniform and trench coat, the only symbols of his authority. He joined a small group called the German Workers' Party, where he was put in charge of propaganda. The party was comparatively unknown, but it made up in noise for what it lacked in strength.

Gustave Landauer formed a Socialist government in Munich and tried to restore some order in the strife-torn city. Buber sat on the platform beside him when he gave a memorial address for two Socialist leaders who had been arrested and murdered in their cells. He spoke of Social Democracy. "Does it not have a Janus head?" he asked. Men of spirit were drawn to it because it represented justice and equality, and at the same time they were repelled by its bureaucracy, its militarism, and its denial of freedom. He quoted a Hungarian poem his wife had translated into German:

> A gentle feeling of anxiety troubles me:
> I would not die on a soft pillow—
> I will not welter in anguish on the cushion,
> Will not slowly droop, melt,
> Like the candle that one forgets in a room,
> Like the flower that a worm eats away.

Landauer had written a book called *The Revolution,* at
Buber's suggestion, in the beginning of their friendship
twelve years ago. In describing the French Revolution
he said: "When a revolution ultimately gets into the terrible situation this one did, with enemies all around it,
inside and out, then the forces of negation and destruction that still live on are bound to turn inwards and
against themselves: fanaticism and passion turn to distrust and so on to bloodthirstiness, or at least to an indifference to the added terrors of killing: and before long
terror by killing becomes the sole possible means to
keep themselves provisionally in power."

Russia and now Germany seemed destined toward
the same mistakes the French had made several generations earlier. "The most fervent leaders of the revolution believed, in their finest hours, that they were leading mankind to a rebirth, but somehow the birth miscar-
ried and they got in each other's way and blamed each
other because the revolution had allied itself to war, to
violence, to dictatorship and authoritarian oppression,
in a word, to politics."

Two weeks after this memorial service, Landauer
called a discussion meeting with some of the revolutionary leaders. The subject he chose was Terror. Again
Martin Buber sat beside his friend, who, he noticed, was
in an unusually quiet mood, only listening to what the
others said, without taking part. The discussions turned
out to be mostly between Buber and a former officer of
the German Army, now a Communist revolutionary.
He still wore his uniform, and he had walked into the

room with spurs clanking. It was expected of Buber, he knew, to speak about the moral issue of terror, but he talked instead about the relation between ends and means, bringing in past revolutions and examples of the present. The former officer defended the use of terror. "Dzerzhinski, head of the Cheka, could sign a hundred death sentences a day, but with an entirely clean soul," he said.

"That's the worst of all!" Buber exclaimed. "This 'clean soul' you do not allow any splashes of blood to fall upon. It is not a question of 'souls' but of responsibility." The officer, with an air of unruffled superiority, merely looked at him as if the remark were not worthy of a reply. When Landauer quietly touched Buber's hand, Buber felt his friend's whole arm quivering.

That was in February 1919. In May of that year Gustave Landauer was assassinated. His Socialist government was replaced by a second Communist revolutionary government, with the former army officer taking a leading part. This barbaric murder of his friend marked another turning in Martin Buber's life. He found himself compelled to think only of that, to picture it in his mind. Not in an optical sense alone, he said, but with his whole body. Oh, something has been done to me, he thought. He felt that from then on, in his meetings with people, especially with the young, he must give more than an exchange of thoughts and feelings. "I had to give the fruit of an experience," he said.

In June Germany sent her representatives to Paris, near where, in the historic Palace of Versailles, they signed the most humiliating peace treaty in the nation's history. She gave up Alsace and Lorraine to France, lost the use of her mines in the Saar Valley, ceded large parts of territory to Poland and Czechoslovakia, with a Polish Corridor cutting off the eastern part of Prussia from the rest of Germany. All German colonies were taken over by the Allied countries. The mercantile fleet was surrendered; the navy had become practically non-existent under the terms of the armistice; and the army was reduced to nothing but a police force. Added to this, the country was faced with an indefinite war indemnity. Austria fared little better, losing most of what was left of her once large empire. Lemberg again became part of Poland.

The bitterness of defeat turned all Germany into a battleground. Regional governments were taken over by revolutionaries, then antirevolutionaries, with as much violence on one side as on the other. One regime became known as the Red Terror, and its successor was called the White Terror.

That autumn Martin Buber went by train to a city a short distance away. Though he had arrived at the railway station early, there was not a vacant seat to be found. He went from carriage to carriage till, in a compartment filled with men in uniform, room was made for him. There was a noisy political discussion going on. Buber heard the name Landauer, and looked up for a glimpse of the speaker. One of the soldiers, a man of about middle age with a reddish beard, was saying,

"No, it was not so with Landauer. Landauer wanted the right thing. If only he had been one of us!"

During these unsettled times the question must often have been asked in Germany, "What is one to do?" Buber's answer was that one alone could do nothing. He saw no solution in individualism, when man, wrapped in his shell of self, stands forlorn and incapable. Collectivism, the kind that had taken over Russia and was threatening Germany, was no better. Man stood forlorn and incapable also in highly organized masses, where he was out of contact with other individuals. For the ideal community there must be a spirit of genuine dialogue, a direct mutual relation between man and man, he said. *"You shall not withhold yourself* is the old eternal answer, but its truth is new and intact."

In an address to the Twelfth Zionist Congress in 1921, he said: "We have passed from the difficult period of the World War into a period which outwardly seems more tolerable, but on closer examination proves still more difficult, a period of inner confusion. It is characteristic of this period that truth and lies, right and wrong, are mingled in its various spiritual and political movements in an almost unprecedented fashion."

He spoke, as he so often did, in behalf of an understanding between Jews and Arabs in Palestine, and he warned against a false nationalism, the kind that is an end in itself. A concern with supremacy over neighboring nations was destructive. "Not power, but power hysteria is evil," he said.

Life in Munich had become as intolerable as it had been in Berlin. The Bubers found a home in the village of Heppenheim, nestled against the gently rolling hills of the Odenwald. It was a short train ride from Heidelberg and fifty minutes from Frankfurt am Main. From his upstairs study window Buber looked out on a quiet scene of ancient timbered houses with tile roofs weathered to many colors. In the distance he could see, to his right, the spires and towers of St. Peter's Church, pink against the sun's glow. To his left stood Starkenburg Castle. It had been given its name, meaning strong, because it had withstood the siege of every battle fought over this land. The foothills, looming as a backdrop behind the church and castle, sheltered the village in winter, and spring came earlier here than in Munich, farther south.

Here was the tranquillity necessary to a writer and philosopher, and here also was companionship with other philosophers and scholars from neighboring universities and with a new generation of students who came at the visiting hour. One afternoon in December, 1921, Franz Rosenzweig, a man of about thirty-five, came down from Frankfurt with his wife, Edith. He had established an academy of adult education for Jews the year before, and was then translating ancient hymns from Hebrew into German. It was inevitable that the conversation should turn to religion. Rosenzweig had spent the war years in the Balkans and Poland, and had been very much impressed with the East European Jews

A view of the Jewish quarter of Frankfurt at the end of the nineteenth century. (CULVER PICTURES, INC.)

he met. He wanted to talk now of Buber's books on Hasidism.

"It has been surprising that, in all the years since they were published, only one person has written to ask where I obtained my information," Buber said.

Rosenzweig answered that he had been searching all along for the original sources. "I think there are quite a few people, including myself, who have wanted to know, but simply haven't written," he said.

The men and their wives, and two young students who had called that day, sat talking over coffee and cake. Buber mentioned that someday he would like to present the sources of the Hasidic legends to a few interested persons. Rosenzweig immediately spoke up. He could get together those interested persons, though it would have to be in summer, and not during the winter. The group could take hikes in the mornings, and in the afternoon stop off at Heppenheim. "But I'd want to know how you plan to go about it, so I can explain it to the people," he added.

Buber agreed to a trial lesson, with the two students as part of the audience. They moved to another room, and Buber took a few books from the shelves. Referring to one, he talked about the importance and the reality of the word. This was a subject that fascinated him, and he often spoke of it in his writings and lectures. He talked of the coming into being of words as one of the most mysterious processes of the life of the spirit. Once, when a newly founded academy of philosophy announced that its task would be to create new words of spiritual value for Western peoples, Buber answered that it could not be the task of an organization to *make* words. Only a word born in the spirit could be creative in man. The academy should concern itself instead with the purification of the word. "What is needed is not teaching the use of new words, but fighting the misuse of old words."

On his way back to Frankfurt, Rosenzweig thought of the afternoon's conversation. The idea came to him that it would be simpler to transport the prophet than to transport twenty of his disciples. The next day he wrote to Buber, asking if he would consider coming to Frankfurt to give his lectures at the Jewish Academy. "To my own surprise," Buber answered, "though refusing has been second nature to me for many years, I feel disposed to accept your proposal."

In a letter to a friend telling of his visit with Buber, Franz Rosenzweig wrote, "I suddenly realized that he was no longer the mystical subjectivist that people worship, but that even intellectually he was becoming a solid and reasonable man."

This was not his first meeting with Buber. He had called upon him in Berlin seven years earlier, in the spring before the war started. It was just after he had completed his education, with degrees in philosophy and medicine. His interests had then turned to Jewish religious thinking. The year before, he had decided to become a Christian, believing, with many other young Jewish intellectuals, that the age-old problem of dissension could be solved through assimilation and conversion. His conversion must not be as a pagan, but as a

Jew, he had declared. It must be as it was with the first converts at the beginning of Christianity, as with Paul, who had said proudly, "I am a Jew," as with Peter and John, who, after receiving the Holy Spirit, went to the temple at the time of prayer, as with the Twelve who shared with Jesus his last supper, a celebration of the Jewish Passover, in Jerusalem.

On the day before he planned to take this step, he went to the synagogue to pray. It was on the Day of Atonement. He heard the chanting of the Psalms and hymns, and he joined in the age-old prayers. "Hear, O Israel, the Lord our God, the Lord is One." In the crowded synagogue, his voice blending with other voices, the feeling came over him that he stood alone, and in utter loneliness before the Divine Presence. "The Lord is God: the God of Love. He alone is God." There came the sound of the great ram's horn, one long poignant note, a symbol of all that was past, and hope for the future. When the service was over, Franz Rosenzweig walked out of the synagogue knowing that he would never turn from the faith of his people.

This experience was too personal to mention to others, but in their first meeting Buber sensed in the other man an eagerness to know more about the cultural and religious history of the Jews that he had had before taking up his own work on Hasidism. He encouraged the young man to write an article for one of his publications, expressing some of these ideas taking shape.

"Jews and Christians both deny that the ethical and religious principle of 'Love God and thy neighbor' is their common possession," Rosenzweig wrote once in his journal. "Each tries to impute paganism in the other; the Christians by disallowing our love of neighbor, we by disallowing their love of God. Both are right and both are wrong. Here the insincerity of liberal theology becomes apparent."

The meeting of Martin Buber and Franz Rosenzweig was an important event in the lives of both men. "It's marvelous for me, and a great blessing," Rosenzweig wrote after their meeting at Heppenheim. He was then feeling the first slight symptoms of a slow paralysis that would keep him lingering for nine years, completely helpless in body but undaunted in spirit and with a mind as brilliant and alert as ever until the end.

For his first series of lectures in Frankfurt, Buber chose the subject "Religion as Actuality." He brought into these lectures some of the material of a book he was then working on, presenting the philosophy that had been developing since his student days. A change had come into his writing in the last year or so. His style had become more direct, still poetic but with almost biblical simplicity. In giving a name to his philosophy, he chose the simplest of words, the two pronouns *I* and *Thou,* combined as one word. *Ich und Du.* In German the second-person-singular pronoun is used both in reverence and in close intimacy:

> "The primary word *I-Thou* can only be spoken with the whole being.
> The primary word *I-It* can never be spoken with the whole being."

The philosophy of Albert Schweitzer was becoming known and talked about then. The name he gave it, *Reverence for Life,* had come to him, unexpected and unsought, one day at sunset as he was going up the Ogooué River in the heart of Africa. He was on his way to visit the sick in a jungle village, with his mind on the war and the needless suffering and destruction it had brought. A herd of hippopotamuses, bathing in the river ahead of him, suddenly scattered in different directions at the approach of the boat, though any one of them alone would have been a menace to all on board. The thought came to Dr. Schweitzer, "I am life which wills to live, in the midst of life which wills to live." Every living creature had the desire to live, and every living creature had the right to live.

There was a similarity in the two philosophies, *Reverence for Life,* and *I and Thou.* Neither was new. Buber's went back to the Old Testament, to the teachings of Jesus, who saw God's presence in all nature, the lilies of the field, the sparrow that falls, to the Hasidic hallowing of the everyday, to the early Christian mystics. His way of presenting this philosophy, however, was new:

> To man the world is twofold, in accordance with his twofold attitude.
> The attitude of man is twofold, in accordance with the twofold nature of the primary word which he speaks.

The book *I and Thou,* published in 1923, was written as a poem, and, as in all poems, one finds a deeper meaning with each reading. Though it was written simply, Buber was called upon time and again to explain certain thoughts.

In the twofold attitude of man, the *I-Thou* relationship is mutual, direct, personal; the *I-It* relationship is objective, impersonal.

> The spheres in which the world of relation is built are three.
> First, our life with nature, in which the relation clings to the threshold of speech.
> Second, our life with men, in which the relation takes on the form of speech.
> Third, our life with spiritual beings, where the relation, being without speech, yet begets it.

Two men, friendly and in complete agreement, might enter into conversation, but unless they are wholly together in spirit and there is true dialogue between them, the relation can only be *I-It*. On the other hand men may sit together in silence with true communication that has no need for words, and the relation is *I-Thou*. Or strangers even, with a brief exchange of glances as they pass each other, may reveal a bond of mutuality.

God is the eternal, all-embracing Thou, with whom one can commune and of whom one knows nothing. We are able to talk *to* Him, but not *about* Him. Here, too, the communion must be without reserve, with all one's being, or the attitude becomes objective, impersonal, an *I-It* relation.

Buber wrote of man's twofold attitude toward animals and things, and of the rare occasions when it becomes *I-Thou*.

Sometimes I look into a cat's eyes.

Animals do not communicate with human beings in their glance, he said, however much their owners like to think so. Their look is one of indifference or anxiety. But once in a great while there comes, for only an instant, something in the glance that had not been there before, something he described as a quality of amazement and questioning: "Is it possible that you think of me? Do you really not just want me to have fun? Do I concern you? Do I exist in your sight? Do I really exist? What is it that comes from you? What is it that surrounds me? What is it that comes to me? What is it?"

Immediately the spell is over, and the world of *It* returns. But for the space of a glance the world of *Thou* had shone out from the depths, only to be extinguished and put back into the world of *It*.

I consider a tree.

Buber described the many ways he could look upon a tree. He could see it as a picture, "stiff column in a shock of light, or a splash of green shod with the delicate blue and silver of the background." He could see the tree as movement: "flowing veins on clinging, pressing pith, suck of root, breathing of leaves, ceaseless commerce with earth and air—and the obscure growth itself."

A tree could be classified, it could be measured, it could be counted as one among a number of others, and the tree would still remain an object, existing in the realm of *It*.

"It can, however, also come about, if I have both will and grace, that in considering the tree I become bound up in relation to it. The tree is now no longer *It*. I have been seized by the power of exclusiveness."

One does not have to give up the other ways of looking at a tree to reach this attitude. All these things—picture, movement, classification, measurement, number—were united in this experience.

"Everything belonging to the tree is in this: the form and structure, its colors and chemical composition, its intercourse with the elements and with the stars, are all present in a single whole.

"The tree is no impression, no play of my imagination, no value depending on my mood, but it is bodied over against me and has to do with me, as I with it—only in a different way.

"Let no attempt be made to sap the strength from the meaning of the relation. The relation is mutual."

The *Thou* cannot be found through seeking. It meets us through grace, and we step into direct relation with it. "Hence," Buber said, "the relation means being chosen and choosing. . . ." This relation, into which we have entered with our whole being, cannot be sustained long. We must return time and again to the world of *It*.

In all seriousness of truth hear this: without It man cannot live. But he who lives with It alone is not a man.

6 THE PRODUC-TIVE YEARS

ON HIS DAYS IN FRANKFURT, MAR-TIN BUBER OFTEN SPENT THE TIME BETWEEN LECTURES WITH THE Rosenzweigs in their attic apartment on Schumann Street. As he climbed the stairs his thoughts must have been a mixture of anxiety over his friend's failing condition and admiration for his tremendous will. For the first few months after his attack, Franz Rosenzweig had kept on with his teaching, though instead of going to the academy, he had the students come to him. His landlord gave him the use of one of the large rooms in the house for the lectures, and the seminars were held in his study. Eventually this too had to be given up as the

107

paralysis began to affect his speech so that he was no longer able to make himself understood.

Every morning, with the help of his wife and a servant, he was able to make his way from the bedroom to his study. There, seated at his desk, surrounded by his many books, he managed to accomplish an amazing amount of work, writing articles, personal letters that were essays in themselves, translating Hebrew poetry into German, though keeping the rhythm and meter of the original language.

He chose his successor as director of the academy, and, with a mind as keen as his body was helpless, he kept up his interest, giving advice and instructions whenever he was called upon. The Free Jewish Academy was one of many small academies in Frankfurt, but it was unique in its method of teaching, under Rosenzweig's direction. There were lecture courses and study and discussion groups in Jewish religious history, theology, the Bible, Hebrew language and literature.

By 1923, the year Buber's *I and Thou* was published, Rosenzweig had lost the use of his hands and could no longer communicate by writing down his thoughts. His wife, who understood better than anyone his faltering, mumbled words, wrote as he dictated, for his visitors to read and answer.

One Thursday in January of that year, Martin Buber sat with him, discussing plans of the Frankfurt University to establish lectureships on the three religions, Catholic, Protestant, and Jewish. Buber did most of the talking, telling of his opinion on how the Jewish lectures should be conducted. In Rosenzweig's eyes there was an expression of understanding and agreement. Now and then he tried to speak, but it was too difficult. A day or so later, Buber received a letter of many pages that Rosenzweig had dictated to his wife:

"I could not talk to you about the matter I now take up in this letter because it requires a rather epic scope. It is of some importance, and you inadvertently gave me quite a number of suggestions in the course of conversation. So listen quietly, and remember that I am aware of the objections and nevertheless consider it necessary to propose the matter to you. I have thought it over for weeks."

In the early spring of the previous year he had been asked to take over the new lectureship at the university, on Jewish religious philosophy and ethics, and he had accepted. The paralysis had not progressed far at that time, and he had hoped to be able to lecture for one semester at least, to set the course on the right track, but the official appointment, which had to be issued by the central government in Berlin, had not come through until a month ago.

"I should now like you to consider whether you can take over this task," he wrote to Buber. The whole matter was in the stage when anything could happen to it. In the wrong hands it could be turned into nothing more than another institution among many, for training rabbis. Buber, he said, with his personality and liberal outlook, was the one who could prevent this. The letter ended with, "What I wanted to say to you yesterday and could not: those were lovely days." Buber found himself saying yes to this request as he had to the first one over a year ago.

Frankfurt, though taking pride in the fact that it was the birthplace of Goethe, was a commercial center, where for centuries merchants from all over Europe had come twice a year, in spring and autumn, to the International Trade Fair. The university was scarcely nine years old when Martin Buber agreed to become part of the faculty. It had struggled through the war years and aftermath of defeat, yet its enrollment was growing and the number of its courses increasing.

Germany at that time was going through one of the worst depressions of its history. Commerce had become little more than barter. Goods were available and jobs were plentiful, but money had become worthless. The mark, which had been worth twenty-four cents before the war, had been going steadily down until it reached a value of 24 trillionths of a cent. It was no longer counted but measured, so many million marks to a centimeter. A woman going to market or a man buying a railroad ticket was weighed down by the bag containing the money needed.

On the day of Buber's visit to Rosenzweig in January, the country was faced with another of its many crises. France, impatient at the delay in the heavy reparations payments, sent in an army to occupy the Ruhr, Germany's last and richest coal-mining region.

The people, wearing clothes bought before the war,

mended and kept as clean as possible, read the news on bulletin boards or in their daily paper, stunned and apprehensive. This was the kind of incident that fomenters of dissension thrive on.

In Munich, Adolf Hitler had been biding his time. Now, here was the opportunity he had been waiting for. His reputation had been slowly growing, especially among the uprooted former soldiers. "When the day comes for us to march, no soldier and no policeman will shoot at us. For that day, prepare yourselves," he had said to them. When the French took over the Ruhr, he decided that day had come. On the pretense of dedicating a flag, he planned a march down the city streets with five thousand of his men, known as storm troopers because of their tactics of violence. But the Bavarian government was still strong enough to oppose him. He was refused a permit for his parade. In vain he pleaded with the minister and with the police president, promising on his word of honor there would be no riots. When that didn't succeed he made threats. With or without permission he would march with his men, and he would be at the head of the parade. If the police fired, he would be the one shot down. The government's answer to that was that there would not only be no parade but that the public meetings at which Hitler was scheduled to speak were banned. Again Hitler had to wait, this time for nine months.

On the evening of November 8 a meeting was held in a large hall called the Beer Cellar. About three thousand people were gathered around rough-hewn tables, drinking beer from stone mugs and listening to political speeches. When Adolf Hitler arrived and stood outside the entrance, he might have been taken for one among the many guests, though a close observer would have seen two burly bodyguards, one on each side, and a group of followers surrounding him. Three thousand storm troopers had quietly assembled in Munich, with six hundred of them quietly taking up their posts outside the hall.

The Bavarian prime minister was on the platform, reading his speech, when Hitler charged into the room, jumped on a chair, and shot a pistol into the air. His voice, like the scream of a madman, broke the stunned silence: "The national revolution has begun!" Outside the door his men had set up a machine gun, and the storm troopers held their rifles at ready. Three government officials, including the police chief, were taken and held as hostages.

At first the insurrection appeared successful, but before the night was over the crowd, confused and scarcely knowing what to do, gradually broke up and left the hall, one or two at a time. The next morning the assembled storm troopers, rowdy young adventurers and plunderers, wearing windbreakers and Norwegian ski caps, began a march toward the center where the government buildings stood. Under the swastika banners they goose-stepped, with loaded rifles, some with bayonets, across their right shoulders. They came to a bridge on the Isar River where a police squad was stationed to bar the way. The marching men fell on the police, grabbed their guns, spat on them, and struck them in the face.

It was the march of Adolf Hitler's dreams. He led the way, with the war hero General Ludendorff marching beside him, while he, the corporal, gave orders. Down the narrow streets they went, some of the men singing to keep time to the tramp of their feet, until they reached the open plaza of the city's center. There they found another police squad, of a hundred men, barring the way.

A shot was fired, and others followed. After a minute or so that seemed an eternity, it was all over. Fourteen of the storm troopers lay dead in the streets. The others, seeing that their leader had disappeared, scattered and broke into a run.

A few days later Hitler was captured and sentenced to five years in prison for high treason. News of the Beer Hall Putsch spread over the world, and press reporters from every important country came to the trial and demanded interviews. Though his insurrection had been a failure, Hitler enjoyed the publicity he received. In prison he began work on a book he called *Mein Kampf.* A former book, *Adolf Hitler, His Life and Speeches,* was little known outside his group of followers. This new book, with its message of racism, bitterness, and threats, must reach out over the whole country:

"How long can this process of race betrayal go on? It can go on until from out of this mass one man suddenly rises up, who seizes the leadership, and little by little fans the rage of the people, which so far has been restrained, into a flame against the betrayers."

Mein Kampf was brought out only a few months after the publication of *I and Thou,* with its message of unity:

"He who goes out with his whole being to meet his *Thou,* and carries to it all being that is in the world, finds Him who cannot be sought."

Hitler's five-year sentence was suspended after he had served eight and a half months, but he was warned against making any more public speeches for a certain period of time. He emerged from prison to find a relaxed and stable Germany. France's allies, England and the United States, had strongly disapproved of the occupation of the Ruhr. Even the French people, weary of years of war and bloodshed, elected a new parliament that was opposed to this or any other act of aggression. Furthermore, a committee of American and British bankers drew up a plan, known as the Dawes Plan, to restore Germany's currency and put it on a sound basis. And a limit was set on the reparations payments.

Hitler's following had dwindled to only a handful by the time he came out of prison. The French had already begun to leave the Ruhr. Money flowed into Germany from English and American banks. All over the country there were signs of rebuilding, with jobs for all at stable wages. Food and fuel were plentiful again, and even a few luxuries were coming in. Once-belligerent nations were now friendly, and the books that were popular in England, Germany, and America were those proving the war had been a mistake on both sides. It was in the past now, and best forgotten along with the hardships and turmoil that had followed.

"Believe me the time will come," Hitler said to the few who listened to him. "The illusory foundations of our economic life will again vanish beneath our feet and then perhaps people will understand our words better than now."

He vowed never to attempt another insurrection. He would work from within the government by using the weapon of the Communists—propaganda. With propaganda he would win over the masses. With propaganda he would influence those in high office or, failing in that, see that his sympathizers were elected in their place.

"Go to the masses!" he shouted to those who remained with him.

An international educational conference was held at Heidelberg to discuss the development of the creative powers in the child. Martin Buber was asked to be one of the speakers.

"Future history is not inscribed already by the pen of a casual law on a scroll which merely awaits unrolling," he said. "Its characters are stamped by the unforeseeable decisions of future generations. The part to be played in this by everyone alive today, by every adolescent and child, is immeasurable, and immeasurable is our part if we are educators. The deeds of the generations now approaching can illuminate the gray face of the human world or plunge it in darkness."

In the spring of that year, 1925, he was asked by a Berlin publisher to make a translation of the Old Testament. The fifteenth-century translation made by Martin Luther was still the best in the German language. Buber agreed on condition that Franz Rosenzweig could collaborate with him on it. The following Wednesday, the day of his lectures at the university, he called on Rosenzweig to tell him about the proposal. He sensed from the younger man's expression that he was both pleased and disturbed. It was not until later that Buber understood the reason. Rosenzweig had come to realize early in the course of his illness that he would not go quickly, but would linger on, living in the uncertainty of how much time he had left. He saw in Buber's proposal a project that would take years of intense study and work. That meant readjusting his thinking in terms of the future.

"Let's try it." His lips formed the words his wife interpreted for him.

"Which chapter?" Buber asked.

"The first."

They started at once on the translation of Genesis. Buber made the first draft, which he mailed to Rosenzweig, who went over it, making suggestions, and sometimes, perhaps, objecting to a word or phrase and offering another in its place. Buber either accepted the suggestions that he felt were an improvement over his interpretation or he would explain his reason for his choice of words in translating the passage. To spare his friend efforts in research, he cited various controversial interpretations from the earliest commentators to the latest essays in scholarly journals.

Both men felt the importance of keeping to the spirit of the original Hebrew. This history of a people and their God had been handed down orally from generation to generation before there was a written language. Sometimes the heroic deeds were chanted. The natural pauses for breath in the spoken word, the melody of the poetry, which in Hebrew depends upon accent rather than upon a given number of syllables, and the characteristic repetitions for emphasis were all faithfully kept in the translation.

When the first draft was completed, with its many corrections and changes, Buber began the final copy for the printer. Here again there were discussions and new suggestions on the proofs. Wednesday became known as "Buber day" in the Rosenzweig household. Together the men went over any controversial matters that could not be solved by mail. The corrected proof was read to them together, after which they compared notes, and again there were discussions. With the third proof approved, the book was ready for the press. They worked in this way for five months before the book of Genesis was finished. Rosenzweig wrote a poem in celebration which he sent to Buber:

> I have learned
> That every beginning is an end.
> Quit of the task of writing, I wrote,
> " 'Into Life.' "
> After scarcely two years
> The hand ready for work grew lame,
> The tongue ready for speech stood still,
> So only writing was left me.
>
> But this end became a beginning for me:
> What I wrote
> Has not—thanks to you, dear friend,—
> Remained mere writing.
> We have written the Word of the Beginning,
> Prime act that pledges the meaning of the end.
> And thus the Holy Writ began.

Rosenzweig had been asked to write about Martin Buber for an encyclopedia, the *Jewish Lexicon,* soon after the beginning of their collaboration, but he found he could not. "To portray you, to write 'about' you is something I can't do," he wrote to Buber. Rosenzweig felt he could write about friends he had known longer because, since his illness, he was no longer, or very seldom, able to write to them. "But you, who entered on the 'seventh day of the feast,' are still too much new (and ever again new) a face for me to be able to portray you before the public. I must leave it at the fleeting image on my retina, and I hope it will not change while I live."

When Genesis was finished and in the hands of the publisher, they immediately started work on the book of Exodus. One book followed another, all translated with the same painstaking care as the first. Sometimes the choice of a single word would be the subject of weeks of correspondence. The two commandments of the Old Testament that Jesus called the greatest of them all were translated as "Love God with all your might" and "Love your neighbor as one like yourself." The earlier translation, "Love your neighbor as yourself" gives the wrong impression, Buber explained. "In reality one does not love oneself, but one should rather learn to love oneself through the love of one's neighbor to whom, then, I should show love as I wish it shown to me." In these two separate commandments, both God and the neighbor, meaning, not man in general, but one whose life crosses ours, are to be loved, but in different ways. One is to love God with all one's might and soul. "God limits Himself in all His limitlessness. And in our boundless love for Him, He makes room for love to his creatures."

Most of the modern translations of the Bible have lost the poetic quality of the original while trying for exactness. In this work as much attention was paid to one as the other. The lines in Isaiah 28:16, known to English readers as "Behold, I lay in Zion for a foundation a stone, a tried stone, a precious corner stone, a sure foundation," were translated into German with the same play of words as in the Hebrew. "I will found in Zion the precious corner stone of a founded foundation." This threefold repetition was, according to Buber, to emphasize the decisive quality of the verb.

On his weekly trips between Heppenheim and Frankfurt, Martin Buber could see from his train window the well-kept public forests, and the newly restored suburban houses along the way. Beyond the forests were farm lands divided into small plots and rented to laborers from town. Every summer evening after the work in shops and factories was over, the whole family, husband, wife, children, grandparents, took the long hike to their garden. There they planted and cultivated fruit trees, grapes, berries, vegetables or flowers, making the most of every inch of earth. They brought their supper of bread, sausage, and wine in large baskets, and ate picnic style. There was a comradeship among these landholders. On holidays they strung paper lanterns that stretched from one plot to the other, and they feasted together. They made a strong drink for their celebration with bottles of wine poured over a fermentation of fruit, sugar, and brandy, and the sound of their jolly drinking songs floated through the windows of every passing train. The past was forgotten, with its war and hardships, and the future loomed bright and carefree before them. There was a spirit of optimism over the whole country, from laborer and peasant to the heads of government.

These were Martin Buber's most productive years. On February 8, 1929, he celebrated his fiftieth birthday. His friends got together an anniversary volume containing articles written for the occasion. It was edited by Franz Rosenzweig, whose contribution was a discussion of one of the passages from Buber's doctoral thesis. For Paula Buber, there was a gift equally treasured, a poem from her husband, "On the Day of Look-ing Back," in which he expressed the depth of their relationship.

By this time the first eight books of the Bible were fin-ished, and work was started on the ninth, the book of Samuel. Both men agreed it was a tremendous job. "The hardest of my life," Buber called it. There was hardly a book in the Old Testament whose text had been so tampered with, Rosenzweig said in a letter to a friend. Knowing this, and yet wanting to keep everything worth keeping, was what made the work so difficult.

Franz Rosenzweig's paralysis was growing steadily worse and it seemed that sheer willpower alone kept him alive. When he could no longer use his voice, he communicated by what he called the alphabet method. His wife, or sometimes one of the nurses, recited the al-phabet, beginning with *A*. Rosenzweig indicated the correct letter by the expression of his face or by a barely perceptible movement of the left hand, which still had a trace of feeling. In this way word by word was spelled out. Sometimes his wife knew instinctively after the first letter or so which word would follow, and at times she was able to answer a question for him, judging from his features whether or not she was right.

During the time he was working with Rosenzweig on the translations, Buber was busy with many other inter-ests. He, a Catholic theologian, and a Protestant physi-cian and psychotherapist, published a journal together, *The Creator,* showing how shared religious understand-

ing could be applied to social and educational problems. He was writing on a variety of subjects then. Even
the answer to a questionnaire sent to him could result in
an essay. Yet in all his writings and lectures the same
philosophy was repeated, the relationship of God and
man and nature. He brought out another book from his
research on Hasidism, called *The Hasidic Books*.

As his reputation grew, Buber was more and more in
demand as a lecturer. He traveled throughout Germany, lecturing in Kiel, in Munich, Heidelberg, Berlin.
At Heppenheim he spoke at a meeting of Catholics,
Protestants, and Jews on how religion could help in
bringing about social progress. And in Frankfurt he
gave a talk, "China and Us," at the Sessions of the
China Institute. Twice he appeared on the lecture platform with Albert Schweitzer. A cherished memory remained with both men, never to be forgotten, of hours of
walk and talk together in mutual understanding.

In Prague, where Buber had been invited to lecture,
he met Rabindranath Tagore, the Indian poet and philosopher, who was visiting in the home of a professor of
Sanskrit. Tagore wanted to discuss the problem of Zionism and the Jewish settlement of Palestine. Wasn't there
danger, if the Jews became a nation, that they would
lose that reverence for the spirit and universalism? he
asked. Wouldn't it result, rather, in a narrow-hearted
nationalism and materialism?

There was this danger, Buber agreed. With nations as
well as with individuals, dangers threatened at certain

stages. The way to overcome them, however, was not by turning away, but by recognizing them and directing one's forces against them. It was possible to fill Zionism with that inherited treasure, reverence for the spirit and universalism. And it was also possible, Buber went on, in the settlement of Palestine and for the Oriental peoples as a whole, to learn from the west its positive values, and at the same time reject its inner disorder and lack of direction.

Tagore nodded, but Buber saw that he was not wholly in agreement. The West was too powerful, in spite of its signs of degeneration, he argued, for one to accept it and at the same time protect oneself against it. Its materialism should be opposed by the genuine meditation of the East. One must prove the emptiness and meaninglessness of turmoil in the West, and turn it, together with the Orient, toward a search for the eternal truth.

Buber answered Tagore with a parable. Imagine a man climbing a mountain, carrying a heavy sign to plant at the top, he said. When the man has struggled halfway up, he meets someone who is puzzled over this seemingly senseless burden. "Throw it down and you'll find your climb easier," he advised. "Not so," the man replied. "I am climbing upward in order to plant this sign at the top." And so it was with the human spirit, Buber explained. It cannot throw off the burden of its civilization, for inside it a higher value is hidden, which will only shine forth when it emerges from the depths of inner conflict to the pure summit air of justice and peace.

"And the Jews?" Tagore asked.

The Jews were the most exposed point of modern mankind, Buber answered. "We must attack the danger directly in order to overcome it. To do this we need your brotherly help."

"Tagore extended his hand to me," Buber wrote afterward, "and what I felt he surely felt, too—that in the midst of all the hazards of the history of the nations there is a fact of facts which endures uninjured—human brotherliness."

It was always good to return home to Heppenheim, no matter how short the trip, back to the family waiting for him. Raphael, who had married and was now separated, lived there with his two small daughters. Once more the house was filled with the sound of children's voices. Often on a pleasant day Martin Buber left his study and joined Paula in the garden. Sometimes they sat on the rounded bench beneath the large mulberry tree and watched the granddaughters at play. Every season had its show of splendid colors, from the early spring tulips of bulbs sent from Holland to summer roses and the dahlias and chrysanthemums of autumn. An occasional lark or warbler swooped down to perch with fluttering wings on the rim of the lily pond to drink. Outside the garden fence was an old fountain in the shape of a lion's head where the townswomen once drew their household water. Now and then a passerby paused with a friendly greeting and passed the time of day, proud of the fact that a celebrity had chosen to live among them.

On October 24, 1929, startling news came over radios and appeared in the headlines of newspapers. In America, the most stable and productive of countries, the bottom had dropped out of the stock market. Some rejoiced at the news, seeing it as proof that capitalism had failed. Others had a sense of foreboding. Most of the people of the world, however, were then unaffected, and they turned the pages of their paper to other news. America was a wide ocean away from both Europe and Asia, and that country's affairs were her own. On the little garden plots seen from the train window between Heppenheim and Frankfurt, the workers harvested their crops and made plans for a celebration of thanksgiving. For four years Germany had had peace and a growing prosperity, and there was no reason to believe it would not last.

In their translation of the Bible, Buber and Rosenzweig had reached the book of Isaiah, and were almost two-thirds of the way through. One morning, in the early part of December, Edith Rosenzweig, at a signal from her husband, took up the copybook they used for correspondence with Buber, and wrote, as the words were spelled out: "And now it comes, the point of all points, which the Lord has truly revealed to me in my sleep: the point of all points for which there—" They were interrupted by the doctor's visit, and the letter was put aside, never to be finished. That night Franz Rosenzweig died in his sleep. He had a simple burial, as he had long ago requested, with no funeral oration. At the graveside Martin Buber read one of the Psalms from the Hebrew Bible:

> "Truly God is good to Israel, even to such as are of a clean heart.
> But as for me, my feet were almost gone; my steps well nigh slipped.
>
> Nevertheless I am continually with thee: thou hast holden me by my right hand.
> Thou shalt guide me with thy counsel, and afterward receive me to glory.
> Whom have I in heaven but thee? and there is none upon earth that I desire beside thee.
> My flesh and my heart faileth: but God is the strength of my heart, and my portion forever."

7 FLIGHT TO PALESTINE

THE GREAT DEPRESSION SPREAD LIKE AN EPIDEMIC FROM THE UNITED STATES TO THE REST OF THE WORLD, AFFECTING THE RE-motest of places. Banks were failing everywhere, tenants were evicted, mortgages foreclosed, and millions of workers were out of jobs. Heads of families forgot their pride and accepted government doles, and long lines of hungry people stood before soup kitchens, waiting patiently for something to eat.

Germany, so recently lifted out of one depression, was now sunk in another. Jobs had been plentiful in the first one, but the money earned was practically worthless. In this one jobs and money both were scarce. Hitler had been waiting for just such conditions. In the 1928 elections his party had won only 12 out of 600 seats in the Reichstag, in spite of the violent tactics of his young followers: demonstrations, street fights, invasion of political meetings to shout down their opponents. In the 1930 elections, when the Depression was beginning to be felt, the Nazis won 107 seats in the Reichstag, with a vote of six million.

With each lowering in wages, each factory shut down, each industry forced into bankruptcy, Hitler gained new supporters, men desperate for any change from the intolerable conditions they endured. To those who still remembered the bitterness of defeat he gave hope for a mighty nation rising as a leader among other nations. To those who searched for work and found none he made promises of prosperity and national glory. The youth, especially, were drawn by his fiery, almost hypnotic speeches. He taught them arrogant pride in their race, and hate for other races and beliefs. The two main targets for the hate he fostered were Marxists and Jews, on whom he placed all the blame for Germany's condition.

As early as 1930 many Jews, with a premonition of what was to come, began leaving the country. Others, like the Bubers, chose to remain, keeping on with their way of life in the hope that order and sanity would return to the nation.

"It behooves both of us to hold inviolably fast to our own true faith, that is, to our own deepest relationship to truth," Martin Buber said that year in a speech he gave to a group of Christians in Stuttgart. "It behooves both of us to show a religious respect for the true faith of the other. This is not what is called 'tolerance'; our task is not to tolerate each other's waywardness but to acknowledge the real relationship in which both stand to the truth. Whenever we both, Christian and Jew, care more for God Himself than for our images of God, we are united in the feeling that our Father's house is differently constructed than our human models take it to be."

The Jew experiences as a person what every openhearted human being experiences as a person, he explained. "The experience, in the hour when he is most utterly forsaken, of a breath from above, the nearness, the touch, the mysterious intimacy of light out of darkness."

The two years that followed brought, not the order and sanity that had been hoped for, but deeper depression and a despair that closed the people's eyes to the real danger. In the 1932 elections Hitler had enough support so that he felt strong enough to run for president of Germany against the aging Hindenburg, then eighty. Though he lost the election, his party was powerful enough to bring pressure to bear on the government so that in January, 1933, Hindenburg appointed Adolf Hitler chancellor. Scarcely a month later the Reichstag building was destroyed by fire. A Dutch Communist was accused and executed. Whether the fire was actually set by the Communists or by the Nazis, as many believed, it served Hitler's purpose. He convinced the president that another election should be held. In this one his party gained enough seats so that when the Reichstag assembled at their temporary quarters in Potsdam, a bill was passed giving Adolf Hitler full powers. At the death of Hindenburg, in 1934, the offices of president and chancellor were merged. For twelve terrifying, violent years the Nazis were the sole party in power, with Hitler at its head. Freedom and justice gave way to oppression. Before the end of his rule there would be, aside from the casualties of a second world war, twelve million civilians, men, women, and children—seven million of them Christians and five million Jews—put to death.

The persecutions began first with the Marxists and other political opponents, including, even, Hitler's own men who dared criticize him. The campaign of hate then turned on the Jews. Once-respectful shopkeepers became surly with Jewish customers. Youths with the swastika emblem in their lapels flashed menacing looks. Former friends turned aside in embarrassment, with now and then the noble exception of some who risked their own safety to give help and sympathy. A decree was issued excluding all Jewish students from government-controlled schools and universities.

The memory must often have come to Martin Buber of the story his grandmother used to tell about the demon who drove away the true king and ruled in his stead. The question was still unanswered: Couldn't the people recognize the demon for what he was and go in search of the true ruler?

For five years the Bubers remained in Germany under Hitler's régime. When Jewish students were excluded from the universities, Martin Buber resigned from the faculty at Frankfurt. He became director of the Jewish Academy that Franz Rosenzweig had established. He was also made director of the Central Office of Jewish Adult Education in Berlin. The purpose of this organization was to train teachers for the greatly needed schools for Jewish students throughout the country.

It was said of Buber at this time that he fought the evils of Nazism with patriarchal dignity. Many a despondent Jew, unable to leave, found in him a source of comfort and encouragement. He was especially concerned about the youth, and most of his public speeches were addressed to them. He spoke of that noblest happiness of youth, the happiness of believing in the spirit. There is a truth over and above political parties, above those who wield and are greedy for power.

God carries on His dialogue with all His creatures, even with the one to whom He has given power, and this creature must give an account as to how he has used his power. But God also carries on a dialogue with those who suffer from the abuse of this power. "God does not remain fixed above, from whom irresponsible potentates receive continual installments of authority. When they act contrary to the pact, when they afflict a creature entrusted to them, and this creature sinks to the ground, then God is no longer up above, but down below on the ground beside the afflicted." When Hagar, afflicted by Sarah, was sent off to die in the wilderness, God had come down to her on her own level in the shape of a messenger, and comforted her, Buber reminded his listeners. He quoted from one of the Psalms: "For He is nigh unto them that are of a broken heart."

There were no doubt many in his audiences who, in their tortured last hours, waiting for death in a concentration camp, would find comfort in the memory of these words and of the man who had spoken them. They would have remembered, too, the prayer of one of the early Hasidic masters that Buber repeated to them: "How could I ever venture to ask why everything happens as it does, why we are driven from one exile to another, why our enemies are allowed to torture us! . . . I do not beg of you to reveal the secrets of your way—for I could not endure them. But I implore you to reveal to me with great clearness and profundity what this, which is happening at the moment, means to me, what demands it makes of me, and what you, Lord of the world, wish to tell me through it. Ah, I do not long to know why I suffer, but only if it is for your sake that I suffer."

The Nazis allowed Martin Buber and his family a certain amount of freedom in the early part of the régime. They were able to travel wherever and whenever they wanted. Buber's lectures took him to Belgium and Czechoslovakia, countries soon to be taken over by Hitler's troops. In Prague he lectured on the prejudices of youth. He said that young people think prejudice is something that comes with age, that they themselves are unbiased, but that is not true. The young make their choice vehemently and passionately, before they have gained the experience to judge fairly. Yet older people, too, in spite of their experience, can also be biased. But prejudices are not necessarily bad. There is a kind that strengthens one and leaves him with an open mind so that though he has a definite opinion, he does not shut himself off from the world. And there is the kind that locks a man out of the world and prevents him from seeing anything beyond himself.

The prejudice against God was among those Buber mentioned in his lecture, the most extreme prejudice of all, he called it. In every era men have heard about the death of gods, he said. He told of a story going back to the reign of the emperor Tiberius. Some people on a ship heard a mournful voice call out from one of the Greek islands, bidding the helmsman carry the news that the great god Pan had died. "Whether we know it or not," Buber said, "what we really mean when we say that a god is dead is that the images of God vanish, and that therefore an image which up to now was regarded and worshiped as God can no longer be so regarded and so worshiped."

Throughout the ages man, in his longing for God, has created an image of him in his mind. Again and again he is forced to destroy his image when he sees he has not succeeded, and he builds a better one, more real, more just, more glorious than the last, but this, too, fails. "The images fall, but the voice is never silenced," Buber said to his young audience. "The voice speaks in the guise of everything that happens, in the guise of all world events; it speaks to men of all generations, makes demands upon them, summons them to accept responsibility. I have pointed out that it is of the utmost importance not to lose one's openness. But to be open means not to shut out that voice—call it whatever you will. It does not matter what you call it. All that matters is that you hear it."

Some among his listeners found in Buber a likeness to the zaddik of former years. They had heard tales from parents and grandparents of good men who risked life and freedom to bring comfort to those in despair. It was told of a rabbi that he disguised himself as a drunken thief so he could gain admittance to a barracks prison where a group of conscripts, who had been seized from their homes, were waiting to be sent off to serve in the czar's army. Once inside, he revealed himself to the boys, scarcely more than children, who were huddled together, frightened, weeping. All during the night he talked to them, fighting back his own tears. He reminded them of Joseph who was led away into captivity, and he told of martyrs who had clung to their faith through all their persecutions. He urged them never to forget that eternal prayer glorifying the unity of God: "Hear, O Israel, the Lord our God, the Lord is One."

At dawn the guard came into the room and discovered him. The rabbi arose and said: "Lambs of the God of Israel, I must go now to my punishment. I may not be found worthy of surviving until your return, but in the true world we shall surely meet. May it be the will of God that I shall have no reason to be ashamed of you there, before Him."

For the Jews to whom Buber spoke, the future held one of two things, exile or a concentration camp with possible extermination. "He counseled, comforted, raised their dejected spirits," one wrote of him. "Perhaps not many of those who listened to him survived the fiendish slaughter, but if they perished, they died with a firmer faith in their hearts and a deeper conviction in their minds of their people's spiritual destiny."

The Reichstag passed laws in which the Jews were disfranchised, including those with no more than one grandparent who had Jewish blood, and intermarriage was prohibited. Christians, too, were being persecuted, and the Church was no longer free. Hundreds of clergymen were brought to trial and imprisoned, many to be executed later. Like Mussolini, who wanted to restore the glories of ancient Rome to Italy, Hitler wanted a return to the pre-Christian era in Germany.

In 1935 Martin Buber gave a public address in Berlin. Buber dared to criticize this attempt to reach back toward paganism. Only those who had no understanding of the human spirit's development could believe that to build the future one needed only the pattern of a bygone era. The splendors of paganism belonged to their own time. They had grown spontaneously, involuntarily, and not according to a set of plans. The hand that reaches back can only grasp something negative, for the original stuff of paganism cannot be recaptured, he said.

He spoke of the power of the spirit. Time and again in the course of history the spirit has been attacked by powers that swarmed up from below, yet it not only mastered each attack but also set the brand of its own power on the attackers. "Does the same still hold for our own era?" he asked. And in answer to his own question he added: "Though in one historical era after another the spirit may seem dethroned and exiled, it does not lose its power. Again and again, unexpectedly and un-predictably, it causes what is intrinsic in the course of history through its agents, faithful courage and faithful love."

After this lecture the German authorities forbade Martin Buber to make any more public speeches. He was not entirely silenced, however, for his writings had not been banned. In totalitarianism he saw the great dreams and the great hopes of mankind become, one after the other, caricatures of themselves. His friend Leonard Ragaz, a Christian Socialist, had said, "Any Socialism whose limits are narrower than God and man is too narrow for us," and with this, Buber agreed. The ideal collectivism was man becoming a fellow to man, he wrote. And this could not develop without a common relation to the divine unity with God, and with man.

In 1936 Buber published a long article, an elabora-tion of a speech he had given in Switzerland three years earlier, under the title *The Question to the Single One*. It was a discussion of Kierkegaard and his philosophy, emphasizing the importance of the individual, the unique or "single one." Again Buber attacked totalitarianism, and compared it with the ideal collective group. When individuals are joined as a people, a family, a society, a vocational group, a companionship in belief, there is a bond of relation, one with the other. But in the totalitarianism of the present time, "the human crisis we are experiencing today," he called it, collectivity had become exaggerated and perverted. Instead of that ideal bond of relation there was a doctrine of serfdom. The individual had become bound in such a way that he lost his personal responsibility. This kind of collectivity could never take the place of the individual in that dialogue of the ages between God and mankind, he stated.

To his surprise this article was not only allowed to be published; it was uncensored. This was certainly proof that it had not been understood by the proper authorities, Buber said.

By 1938 Hitler felt strong enough to take his next step toward world conquest. He made demands on his native Austria for an alliance. His terms were such that the Austrian prime minister refused to accept without a plebiscite. Twenty-four hours before the vote was to take place, Nazi troops marched into Austria, subdued the people, and annexed the country to Germany. Czechoslovakia was next. The German minority group there was encouraged by the Nazis to revolt and press for a return of the Sudetenland to Germany.

The Bubers had gone to Switzerland that year with

the intention of returning to Heppenheim after a short vacation, but some of their German friends wrote, advising them to stay away. Conditions were growing worse, and no one was safe from suspicion. Secret police had been seen watching Buber's house. Their daughter, Eva, and her husband, Ludwig Strauss, one of the young scholars who had been associated with Buber, had already left Germany and settled in Palestine. A quick decision was made for the remainder of the family to join them.

Before the year was up, practically every synagogue in Germany was destroyed, along with many sacred pieces of great antiquity. The Jews, in addition to having their citizenship taken away and being barred from institutes of learning, were no longer allowed in parks, libraries, or museums. Those who wanted to leave the country could still do so, but only by forfeiting everything they owned. Mass arrests had begun of both Christians and Jews. They were sent off to concentration camps to join the ever-growing numbers of prisoners held because of political or religious beliefs.

The prisoners were made to wear small patches of triangular cloth of a color to indicate their status. Red was for political prisoners, lilac for members of Christian sects that opposed war, such as Jehovah's Witnesses; black for asocials, and green for criminals. The Jews wore a patch in the shape of a star, red and yellow for Jewish politicals and black and yellow for Jews guilty of what the authorities called racial offenses.

By the time Martin Buber and his family went into

exile, over half the Jews of Germany had left. Though they had been only 1 percent of the population, they had produced 29 percent of that country's Nobel Prize winners. Many of these were among the 60,000 who had left Germany to find a home in Palestine and build a new life.

The winds of Jerusalem blow from all directions. It is said that every wind in the world comes and prostrates itself unto God in Jerusalem before going to that place to which it is destined. The altars of the synagogues where the Torah is kept, in all other parts of the world, face in the direction of Jerusalem. But here the altar is in the center, for this is the center of the universe, so the holy men have said.

"That great city, the holy Jerusalem, descending out of heaven from God. Having the glory of God: and her light was like unto a stone, most precious, even like a jasper stone, clear as crystal."

In the land of Israel even the direction of a stick lying on the ground has holy significance, some have said, and to the newly arrived Jews every mound of earth and every rock was sacred. It was an exile, a separation from familiar scenes that went back to childhood, and it was also a homecoming, to a place loved and dreamed of through all the generations.

" 'The air of this land makes one wise,' the sages said," Buber, then sixty, wrote. "To me it has granted a different gift, the strength to make a new beginning."

He joined the faculty of the Hebrew University soon after his arrival. In his first course of lectures, as Pro-

fessor of Social Philosophy, he asked, with Kant, the
question "What is Man?" In it he explained the teachings of the great philosophers from Aristotle and Kant
down to the most recent ones. In the unfolding of his
question he pointed out that to understand and know
the whole man one must see him, not as an individual or
as a group, but in the reality of the mutual relation between man and man. "If you consider the individual by
himself, then you see of man just as much as you see of
the moon; only man with man provides a full image," he
said. "If you consider the aggregate by itself, then you
see of man just as much as you see of the Milky Way;
only man with man is a completely outlined form." He
ended his last lecture of the series with this statement:
"We may come nearer the answer to the question what
man is when we come to see him as the eternal meeting
of the One with the Other."

Here in the shadow of the Judean hills, where the ancient language could be heard everywhere, Buber found
himself taking up work on the Hasidic legends, which
he had thought long finished. He went back also to his
translation of the Bible.

Memories of his old life in Europe must often have
come to him, of the friends who had died, Franz Rosenzweig, Gustave Landauer. They had not lived to see the
catastrophe brought to their country. But what about
the others, students, young, eager with questions,
searching for answers? And the contemporary friends,
with whom there had been an ever-fresh dialogue,

through words or letters, or in a shared silence. Had such a one found refuge in exile, or had he stayed on, suffering imprisonment and degradation? The haunting, unspoken question came back again and again. In the dread and uncertainty of their fate, did their thoughts turn to this holy land, and did they find comfort in the words of the Psalms, "As the mountains are round about Jerusalem, so the Lord is round about His people from henceforth, even forever."

From Mount Scopus in the northeastern part of the city, where the squat, flat-roofed buildings of the university and hospital stood, one could see the whole countryside all the way to the Dead Sea, fifteen miles away, a turquoise oval beneath a turquoise sky. "In the Universe there are ten measures of beauty. Nine belong to Jerusalem and one to the rest of the world," it is written. "Whoever has not seen Jerusalem in her glory has never seen a beautiful city."

When David was king the hills were covered with forests and terraced in vineyards and olive groves, and the valleys were green pastures where sheep and cattle grazed. Now it had the beauty of sand and stone and bare hills scarred by erosion and neglect, a scorched and barren beauty, gray and brown and dingy red. It was as though, through all the centuries of foreign rule, Babylonian, Roman, Arab, Turk, and now the British, the land had been waiting, worn and abused, for the return of her lost children.

"If I forget thee, O Jerusalem: let my right hand forget her cunning. If I do not remember thee, let my tongue cleave to the roof of my mouth."

Close to Mount Scopus, on the slopes of the Mount of Olives, there is an ancient cemetery where, some believe, all the dead will be resurrected on the last day, at the end of time. Facing it is Mount Moriah, where Abraham had come prepared to sacrifice his only son in obedience to the command of God: "Take now thy son, thine only son whom thou lovest, even Isaac, and get thee into the land of Moriah." And here, too, Solomon built his Temple, on the place where the Lord had appeared to David his father.

The Temple was built in 960 B.C. and was destroyed by the Babylonians less than four centuries later. A second Temple was built in 520 B.C. "Whoever has not seen the building of King Herod has not seen a handsome building in his life." This too was destroyed when the Romans conquered Palestine. A temple to Jupiter was built on the site, and later the Arabs built a mosque. There is a legend that Mohammed came here mounted on his favorite mare, before his ascension into heaven. The mosque was converted into a church during the Crusades, but when the Turks recaptured Jerusalem it became again a Moslem place of worship.

Through all this there has stood the ruins of one wall, its stones long worn, all that is left of the once glorious Temple of Solomon. Here, close to the western entrance to the wide paved space called the Temple area, generations of pious men have come to pray and mourn Israel's loss. The drops of dew found clinging to the stones in early morning have been called tears shed by the wall itself. And on that most holy day, the ninth day of the month of Tishri, some tell of a white dove that appears in the dead of night and coos sadly with the mourners.

The Zionists had acquired 383,350 acres of land from the Arabs by the time the Bubers arrived in 1938. Much of this land had been owned by wealthy absentee landlords who seldom, if ever, had seen it. The rest was bought from Arab villagers who owned land in common. At first the Arabs, living as they had in Old Testament times, tending their flocks of starving sheep and goats, or scratching the stony earth with wooden plows, never fertilizing, never irrigating it, were glad enough to exchange a part of this land for money. Then gradually they began to take notice of what was happening. They saw the Zionist colonies, their numbers increased from 47 in 1922 to 200 by 1939, standing like oases in the barren land. Beyond the villages of neat, red-tiled houses were orchards and woodlots, fields deep-plowed with tractors, sleek cattle grazing, and flocks of laying hens.

Once the Arabs would have swooped down on these villages to take back what had been theirs, but under the British mandate they could act only in small outlaw groups in border fights. The leaders of the Arab countries formed a league and protested to Britain, with demands for an end to Jewish immigration, and prohibition of any more land transfers. The British government, trying to keep to its tradition of fairness, issued a White Paper that was resented by both sides. It was assumed

that the pledge for a Jewish national home had been ful-
filled. Now there would be a restriction in immigration,
limiting the number of Jews to 75,000 within the next
five years. After that, immigration would be subject to
Arab consent, and land transfers would be allowed only
in certain areas of Palestine. There was a promise that
the mandate would end in ten years, with an independent Palestine.

The Arabs, who had never trusted the British, objected to ten more years of their rule, and the Jews, feeling themselves betrayed, were shocked. With German
control spreading out to neighboring countries, the
need for a national home where the persecuted could
find refuge was greater than ever.

Mahatma Gandhi, who had been asked often about
his stand on Arabs and Jews in Palestine, and the persecution of Jews in Germany, gave his answer in a published statement. His sympathies were all with the Jews,
he declared, then added, "But my sympathy does not
blind me to the requirements of justice. The cry for a national home for the Jews does not make much appeal to
me."

Martin Buber read the statement through, scarcely
believing that this could come from a man of goodwill,
one whom he, with the rest of the world, had admired.
Again and again he took up the article, to see if he had
misunderstood it or had reacted with a kind of collective egoism. But however much he read the words and
thought them over, he could find no interpretation
other than that Gandhi had closed his eyes to the truth.

"Why should not the Jews, like other people of the earth, make that country their home where they were born and where they earn their livelihood?" Gandhi had asked. Jews born in France were French in precisely the same sense that Christians born in France were French, he said. If the Jews have no home but Palestine, will they relish the idea of being forced to leave the other parts of the world where they are settled? Or do they want a double home where they can remain at will?

"If I were a Jew born in Germany and earned my livelihood there I would claim Germany as my home even as the tallest Gentile German may and challenge him to shoot me or cast me in the dungeon. I would refuse to be expelled or to submit to discriminating treatment. And for doing this I would not wait for fellow Jews to join me in civil resistance. I would have confidence that in the end the rest are bound to follow my example. The suffering undergone will bring them an inner strength and joy which no number of resolutions of sympathy passed in the world outside Germany can."

Gandhi compared the condition of the Jews in Germany with that of the Indians in South Africa, calling it an exact parallel. He was convinced that if someone with courage and vision could arise and lead the German Jews in nonviolent action, the winter of their despair could, in the twinkling of an eye, be turned into the summer of hope.

Buber wrote a reply to Gandhi's statement, taking up point by point where he felt the truth had been misinterpreted. "Jews are being persecuted, robbed, maltreated, tortured, murdered. And you, Mahatma Gandhi, say that their position in the country where they suffer all this is an exact parallel to the position of the Indians in South Africa at the time you inaugurated your *nonviolence* campaign. There, you say, the Indians occupied precisely the same place and the persecution there also had a religious tinge. There also the constitution denied equality of rights to the white and black races, including the Asians; there also the Indians were assigned to the ghettoes, and the other disqualifications were at all events almost of the same type as those of the Jews in Germany."

Did the Mahatma know what a concentration camp was like? Buber asked. Did he know of the torments in one, the methods of slow or quick death. If so, how could he possibly have drawn a parallel between the Jews in Germany and the Indians in South Africa? The Indians may have been despised, but they were not outlawed and deprived of their rights. As for *nonviolence* in Germany, there had been many instances of *Satyagraha*. "All honor to those who displayed such strength of soul," Buber said. But such actions had not the slightest influence on their persecutors. Theirs was a martyrdom unobserved, unacknowledged, a martyrdom cast to the winds.

Over forty years ago Gandhi had made a speech in South Africa that Buber now read again and studied. If a Jew in Germany had dared utter one sentence of such a speech, he would be made to pay dearly for it.

Gandhi had brought up two incidents in particular to point out the persecution of Indians. One, that a mob of Europeans had set fire to an Indian village, causing some damage. The other that a mob had thrown burning rockets into an Indian shop. The only other complaint was that three Indian schoolteachers had been arrested for walking the streets after the curfew hour and were not acquitted until some time later.

"If I say that thousands on thousands of Jewish shops in Germany were destroyed and burnt out, you will probably answer that the difference is only one of quantity," Buber wrote. But in regard to the synagogues with the sacred treasures all destroyed, there was no parallel. The Boers and Englishmen could not be accused of injuring anything sacred to the Indians.

There was another difference between the position of Indians in South Africa and the Jews of Germany, Buber pointed out. If Gandhi would think back to his time in Africa, he would remember that for him and his fellow countrymen there was always the great Mother India. He must have taken this so for granted that he was completely unaware of the difference between nations having such a mother—"it may not necessarily be a great mother, it may be a tiny motherkin but a mother nevertheless, with a mother's bosom and a mother's heart—and a nation that is orphaned, or to whom one says in speaking of his country, 'This is no longer your country.' "

When Gandhi was in South Africa, 150,000 Indians were living there, but in India there were over 200 millions. This fact nourished the souls of the 150,000 whether they were aware of it or not, and it gave them strength and courage to live, said Buber. "Did you ask then as you ask the Jews now whether they want a double home where they can remain at will? You say to the Jews that if Palestine is their home they must accustom themselves to the idea of being forced to leave the other parts of the world in which they are settled. Did you also say to the Indians in South Africa that if India is their home they must accustom themselves to the idea of being compelled to return to India? Or did you tell them that India was not their home?"

Gandhi had written in his statement: "It is wrong and inhuman to impose the Jews on the Arabs. . . . What is going on in Palestine today cannot be justified by any moral code of conduct. Surely it would be a crime against humanity to reduce the proud Arabs so that Palestine can be restored to the Jews partly or wholly as their national home."

This touched a sensitive spot with Martin Buber, for he had argued since the beginning of Zionism for mutual friendship and understanding between Arabs and Jews. The Arabs had gained the right to this land through conquest and settlement, as had that other wandering nation, the Jews, to whom the land had once belonged, he explained to Gandhi. These two claims could not be pitted against each other, as just or unjust. Both claims should be understood and honored, and every effort should be made to reconcile them. There must be a possibility of finding some form of agreement.

"For we love this land and we believe in its future: and given that such love and faith are surely present on the other side, a union in the common service of the land must be in the range of the possible. Where there is faith and love, a solution may be found even to what appears to be a contradiction. In order to carry out a task of such extreme difficulty—in the recognition of which we have to overcome an internal resistance on the Jewish side too, as foolish as it is natural—we were in need of the support of well-meaning persons of all nations, and hoped to receive it. Now you come and settle the whole existential dilemma with the simple formula: 'Palestine belongs to the Arabs.' "

God does not give away any one portion of the earth. The conquered land is only lent to the conqueror who has settled on it. And God waits to see what he will make of it. The Jews were not like colonists who had settled other lands. They did not depend on the natives to do the work for them. The land was made fruitful through their own strength, as they plowed, spaded, planted, irrigated.

"But it is not only for ourselves that we desire its fertility. The Jewish farmers have begun to teach their brothers the Arab farmers to cultivate the land more intensively. We desire to teach them further, to cultivate the land with them, to 'serve' it, as the Hebrew has it. The more fertile the soil becomes, the more space there will be for us and for them. We have no desire to dispossess them. We want to live with them."

Gandhi had admitted that the persecution of the Jews

had no parallel in history, that the tyrants of old never went so mad as Hitler seemed to have gone. There was a religious zeal in the way he went about his persecutions. If there ever could be a justifiable war in the name of and for humanity, a war against Germany to prevent wanton persecution of a whole race would be completely justified. "But," Gandhi added, "I do not believe in any war. A discussion of the pros and cons of such a war is out of my horizon or province."

"I cannot help withstanding evil when I see that it is about to destroy the good," Buber wrote in answer to this statement. "I am forced to withstand the evil in this world just as I withstand the evil within myself. I can only strive not to have to do so by force. I do not want force. But if there is no other way of preventing the evil from destroying the good, I trust I shall use force and give myself up into God's hands. . . . If I am to confess what is truth to me, I must say: There is nothing better for a man than to deal justly—unless it be to love. We should be able even to fight for justice—but to fight lovingly."

The world was moving toward its second great war, far more terrifying than the first. In May, 1939, Germany and Italy formed a military alliance, and three months later Germany and the Soviet Union signed a trade pact and a ten-year nonaggression agreement. In September German and Russian troops marched into Poland from opposite directions and divided the country between them. England declared war two days later.

A new word, *Blitzkrieg,* came into being: *Lightning*

War. Violent attacks with great numbers of planes and tanks brought quick victory to Germany and her allies. Rumania and Bulgaria fell to the Russians, and Yugoslavia to Germany. On the Western Front the Germans took Norway, Denmark, then Holland and Belgium. France collapsed, and in June, 1940, German troops marched into Paris, Italy captured Greece, and Japan was on her way to capturing all of Southeast Asia. A year after signing the nonaggression agreement, Germany and Russia were fighting against each other.

Fifty-seven nations were drawn into the war. After six years of fighting, with 37 million dead, victims of battle, bombing raids, and political executions in the totalitarian countries alone, the war ended with the explosion of the atomic bomb on Hiroshima and Nagasaki. In Japan the emperor, speaking to his people for the first time, denied that he was a god. In Italy Mussolini was captured and hanged by his own countrymen. And Hitler, seeing Germany's sure defeat, committed suicide. Once more the German people, awaking as from a nightmare, had to set about rebuilding a nation brought to ruin by its leaders.

To the Jews who had survived the concentration camps, there came again that age-old hope of going back to the land of their fathers. But, with immigration to Palestine limited under the mandate of Great Britain, they had to wait, as displaced persons, until the quota allowed them in.

8 THE FINAL YEARS

PALESTINE HAD BEEN COM-PARATIVELY QUIET DURING THE WAR. VOLUNTEERS AMONG ARABS AND JEWS ALIKE HAD FOUGHT ON THE side of the British. To Martin Buber there seemed a possibility that the two groups could reach some accord. He and a group of men who shared his belief had organized an association called *Ihud,* meaning Unity. It was not a political party. The members were united only in a desire for Jewish-Arab cooperation. They could see no deep animosity between these two related Semitic peoples. The Arabs knew the long association of Judaism and the Jewish people with this land, Buber said. And the Jews recognized the Arab rights in Palestine. They

153

were, after all, the large majority of the country's inhabitants. There were holy places here for them also,
and tombs of their ancestors for many generations back.

The members of *Ihud* called for a Palestine that was
neither a Jewish country nor an Arab country, but a binational country, common to the two people. Each
should have equal freedom and independence, equal
participation in government, and equality of represen-
tation. They found themselves violently opposed by
both sides. The ashes of old hates still smoldered. "We
will fight the war as if there were no White Paper, and
we will fight the White Paper as if there were no war,"
David Ben-Gurion, then head of the Jewish Agency,
had declared when the soldiers of both sides were
united. And four months after the end of the war the
League of Arab States declared a boycott of Zionist
goods. Jewish extremist groups retaliated.

The British authorities, again trying to find an impartial solution, held an Inquiry Commission in Jerusalem
in the early spring of 1946. Martin Buber attended as
one of three representatives of *Ihud*. "Mr. Chairman,"
he said, "it is impossible to survey the problems you are
trying to meet without an understanding of the very
roots of Zionism." As a Zionist of nearly fifty years, he
explained the problems to the commission and offered
suggestions as to how they could be solved. They were
facing something quite different from the usual national
antagonisms, and methods other than political ones
were called for. First, he said, the Jews should be allowed to acquire enough land so they could take up that

earliest form of production, from which they had been separated so long. Second, immigration should be unrestricted, especially for the young. Third, there should be, for the Jewish community, self-determination about their way of life and the form of their institutions, and assurance for their development as a community.

At the same time, Buber warned that one's own independence should not be gained at the expense of another's independence. The Arab peasant must not be ousted from his land, nor should his political status be allowed to deteriorate, for the Arabs had natural rights to the land as the Jews had historical rights. "In such a land it is not fitting for one people to dominate the other." Here again he expressed his belief that not only could the Arabs and Jews live in harmony but also that, together, they could open and develop the country for the good of all.

Later in that same year, Buber went to London to speak at a public meeting arranged by the Council of Christians and Jews, under the sponsorship of the dean of St. Paul's Cathedral. Nine years had passed since he had last seen Europe. "And what years!" he said. The nations were at peace, but it was the peace of sheer exhaustion. On both sides a strength had been lost that was never to be regained. Life was still austere in London, with food rationing and a shortage of living space. Here and there gaping holes and piles of rubble, where once there had been sturdy buildings, were mute reminders of the bombs of war.

In his lecture Buber spoke of the relation between

Christians and Jews, and the attempts made from time to time to separate Christianity from the Judaism of the Old Testament which was the only Scripture of the Church during the first century of its existence. Marcion, a Gnostic from Asia Minor, had been the first. He brought to Rome the doctrine of two Gods, one inferior, the Creator and Judge of the Old Testament, and the other superior, the God whom Jesus revealed. The Church rejected this doctrine in favor of the Trinity, a union of Father, Son, and Holy Ghost in one divine nature. Other attempts to deny the God of the Old Testament followed, the latest being that of Hitler, with his distorted, nonspiritual theory that resulted in the persecution of both Jews and pious Christians.

Buber made the plea he had repeated so often in his speeches and his writings, for unity of individuals and for nations as well. Unity, not division and separation, not an everlasting struggle to the death between sects or classes or nations, is the purpose of creation, he said. "The world of humanity is meant to be a single body, but it is as yet nothing but a heap of limbs, each of which considers itself the entire body."

Here too he spoke of the need for peace in Palestine between Jews and Arabs: "It is no real community if it is not composed of real families and real neighborhoods and real settlements. And it is not a real nation if it does not maintain its truthfulness in true relations as well, the relation of a fruitful and creative peace with its neighbors."

The English translation of *I and Thou* had been published in Edinburgh in 1937. With the exception of this and a book about the Baal Shem Tov, published in 1931 and soon forgotten, Martin Buber's works were little known to the English-speaking world until his visit to London. During the two years following, eight of his books were published in English. The poet T. S. Eliot, speaking of his meeting with Buber in London, called it a rare experience of being in the presence of Greatness.

The next two years also saw the end of Buber's dream of a binational Palestine where Jews and Arabs worked together harmoniously. The British high commissioner's effort to govern impartially brought resentment of both Arabs and Jews. The enmity became then a three-sided one, with violence and retaliation. Great Britain took the matter up with the United Nations. The General Assembly met and voted to end the British mandate, and, with the judgment of Solomon, called for a partition, splitting Palestine into two states, one Arab, one Jewish.

On Friday, May 14, 1948, the British flag was hauled down, General Sir Alan Cunningham, the British high commissioner, left Palestine, and the State of Israel, a dream of two thousand years, became a reality. The ceremony began at four o'clock and was over by sunset, the beginning of the Sabbath when no pious Jew could sign his name or travel on any kind of vehicle. In those two hours a new national anthem was played and a new flag raised.

David Ben-Gurion was sworn in as prime minister, and Chaim Weizmann as president, and a proclamation of independence was issued. The new State of Israel would be based on liberty, justice, and peace, the prime minister said. It would cooperate with the United Nations and uphold the principles of its charter. The holy places of Christians and Moslems would be safeguarded. The nation would strive for peace with the Arabs. "And," Ben-Gurion's voice over the radio went out to the whole world, "the State of Israel will be open for immigration of Jews from all the countries of their dispersion."

It had been long since the Sabbath was ushered in with such rejoicing. The synagogues rang with the Psalms of praise, and there was feasting in even the poorest of homes. The next morning the bombs of the Arabs began to fall. Convoys of troops were approaching from all directions: Saudi Arabia in the south, Egypt in the west, Jordan and Syria in the east, and Lebanon in the north.

"The cleft between the two peoples was split wide asunder. The war raged," Buber said. He was no radical pacifist. He did not believe one must always answer violence with nonviolence. In this he could speak for most, but not all, of his political friends, he admitted. "I know what tragedy implies. When there is a war, it must be fought." In this war, which he called the most grievous of the three for him, he saw everything proceeding with "frightening logical consistency and at the same time with frightening meaninglessness."

There were acts of terrorism that had nothing to do with the war. Arab hordes swooped down and commit-

ted outrages against Jewish villages. "My soul bled with
the sacrifice," Buber said of them. But when a band of
Jewish terrorists wiped out the Arab village of Dir
Yassen, killing 254 men, women, and children, he
spoke of it as "a matter of our own, or my own crime
against the spirit." Ten years later he could still say: "I
cannot think about this without feeling myself guilty.
Our fighting faith in the spirit was too weak to prevent
the outbreak and spread of false demonic teaching."

The United Nations sent Count Bernadotte to act as
mediator. When he was assassinated by Jewish terrorists in Jerusalem, his successor, Ralph Bunche, working
with tact and patience, was able to bring about a cease-
fire. An armistice agreement was signed by Egypt and
Israel in February 1949. Later the other Arab nations,
with the exception of Saudi Arabia and Yemen, signed.

Buber, who had opposed the partition, declared that
there could be no peace that was merely a cessation of
war. "There can only be a peace of genuine cooperation," he said. If they were to truly serve the spirit they
must make good all that was missed. They must free
once again the blocked path to an understanding with
the Arab people.

As a result of the armistice, Jerusalem became a divided city, as Palestine was a divided state. Barbed-wire
barriers separated the older part of Jerusalem, now part
of Jordan, from the new section belonging to Israel. A
narrow passageway connected the two sections, with
armed sentinels standing guard on each side. No Arab
could cross into Israel and no Jew into Jordan, with the

exception of the custodians of the abandoned university buildings on Mount Scopus.

Once more the Bubers were driven from their home. They found a place on the tree-shaded Hovevei Zion, or Lovers of Zion Street. The house, which had been built by an Arab, was of native stone, the same gray-yellow color of the surrounding hills. The doors were painted blue and the window shutters were a pale pink. The garden was as large as the one at Heppenheim, with pines and cedars for shade, and bright tropical flowers gave color throughout the year.

The Israeli government lost no time in building a university in the new city, better even than the one on Mount Scopus, and plans were drawn for another hospital, a museum, and a building for Parliament. When the restrictions on immigration were lifted, Jews from all parts of the world began coming in: Kurdish Jews with turbans and baggy trousers, Nomadic Jews from the Arabian Desert, Jews from China who long ago had fled there to escape Russian persecution, Hasidic Jews with the long side curls, survivors from the concentration camps of Europe. They brought with them the language and culture, and the sanitary customs of the country of their origin. Camps were quickly organized all over Israel to receive them, with community kitchens, first-aid stations, nurseries and kindergartens. The Israeli government asked Buber to establish an Institute for Adult Education to train teachers who would go out to these camps and help integrate the newcomers.

Martin Buber was then seventy. His hair and beard

were white, and he walked with a slight stoop caused by untold hours bent over his desk. Once he had said of an aged philosopher of Germany in whose house he had been a guest, "To grow old is a glorious thing when one has not unlearned what it means *to begin*." This could also be said of Buber. He was old in a young way, as he described his friend, for he knew how to begin.

In 1949 he was invited to speak at the Goethe Bicentennial held in Aspen, Colorado. Albert Schweitzer, another of the invited speakers, made his one and only trip to America for the occasion. Buber's work with the university and with the government in training teachers for the immigrants kept him from attending, but his friend Ernst Simon went as his representative, reading the speech he had written.

Two years later Buber retired from the university and made his long-awaited visit to the United States, where he lectured at some of the leading universities. Large crowds attended, as his philosophy was beginning to have a strong influence on the thinking of Christians and Jews alike. The last lecture was given at Carnegie Hall, a short while before his departure. He was disturbed about the Cold War, and brought it into his speech. He saw the world split into two hostile camps, each considering itself the upholder of truth and its opponent the embodiment of falsehood. There was nothing new in groups, national or political, opposing each other, but now the whole planet was divided, and whoever tried to remain impartial found himself accused by both sides. Now as never before the future of

Martin Buber with students at the University of Judaism in Los Angeles in 1952. Buber is second from the right in the front row. Paula Buber, his wife, is at the far right in the second row. (THE LIBRARY OF THE JEWISH THEOLOGICAL SEMINARY OF AMERICA, NEW YORK).

man as man depended upon a rebirth of dialogue, he said. "If our mouths succeed in genuinely saying 'thou,' then, after long silence and stammering, we shall have addressed our eternal *Thou* anew. Reconciliation leads to reconciliation."

On his return to Israel in 1952, Buber stopped off in Germany to accept the Hanseatic Goethe Prize offered by the University of Hamburg. In September of the following year he was back in Germany, this time in Frankfurt, the city that held so many memories for him, both tender and bitter. There he was given the Peace Prize of the German Book Trade.

He was one of the first of his people to resume relations with that country, and for this he was severely criticized. How could he forgive the monstrous things that had been done? he was asked. Many in Israel objected even to accepting from West Germany the reparations offered of 822 million dollars' worth of raw materials, machinery, ships, and rolling stock. While the debate was going on in Parliament, there was rioting in the streets of Jerusalem, in protest. Ben-Gurion, who had demanded the reparations, resigned as prime minister and went off to live in a settlement in the Negev Desert.

In Frankfurt, Buber found little left of the city he had known. All the central part, with its centuries-old timbered houses, intricately carved and decorated, had been reduced to ashes during the war. Only a portion of a stone house here and there, and the cathedral tower, remained untouched. After they had recovered from the shock of war and defeat, the people went to work to rebuild the city. They kept much of the beauty of the old buildings, adorning the fronts with frescoes and wood carvings, as they had been before. Goethe's house was rebuilt exactly as it was when he had lived there. The furnishings and precious manuscripts that had been stored for safekeeping during the war were back in place. But instead of the narrow, crooked streets, with houses crowded close together, wide avenues were built, and open spaces of gardens and courtyards were kept.

Buber's speech of acceptance was given in the Paulskirche, which had also been rebuilt in its same oblong shape with rounded ends. It had been meant as a church but never consecrated, and was used instead for meetings and exhibitions. As always, before beginning to speak, his eyes searched the audience for Paula. He saw her sitting beside Theodor Heuss, the president of the German Republic. There was the secret communication between husband and wife, an exchange of glances, a barely discernible smile. Then he looked at the man sitting next to her, the one who had replaced Hitler as head of the government. It seemed fitting and somewhat symbolic to him that, after the end of that subhuman creature that called itself the *Führer,* the German people should choose as their leader a man of such trustworthy simplicity.

Like a prophet of old, Martin Buber stood before his audience, condemning the iniquities of the subhuman, yet understanding ordinary frailties. To him it was not a question of forgiving. What had been done—the systematic murder of thousands of his people, indirectly by the German government, directly by its representatives —was something that could not be compared with anything in history. The people responsible for such organized cruelty had removed themselves from humanity to an inhumanity so beyond his conception that not even hatred could come to him, much less an overcoming of hatred. "And what am I that I could presume to forgive!" he said.

With the German people themselves, he had more understanding. A great many knew about the evils of the concentration camps, and did nothing to oppose it. Knowing the weakness of men, Buber said, he could not, in his heart, condemn his neighbor for not wanting to become a martyr. Others knew only through vague rumors of the things that were happening, and they did not inquire further to learn if the rumors were true. These too Buber could understand, for he knew that human dread of knowing what they could not bear to know. There was still another group, those who did know what was being withheld from the people, and dared to protest. Some were given orders and refused to carry them out. These were put to death or, seeing they could do nothing against the monstrous events taking place, put themselves to death. "I see these men very near before me in that especial intimacy which binds us at times to the dead and to them alone. Reverence and love for these Germans now fills my heart."

He spoke of peace. Here in this divided country the cold war between Communism and Democracy was more in evidence than in any other part of Europe. No longer could one travel freely from Dresden to Hamburg, from Leipzig to Heidelberg, or from East Berlin to West Berlin. Again Buber urged a return to genuine dialogue between nations and between people, a dialogue in which each side, though standing in opposition to another, would listen and recognize in his opponent an existing other. He repeated words he had said at the time of the armistice after the Arab-Israeli War. A great peace is something essentially different from the absence of war. "Peoples must engage in talk with one another through their truly human men if the great peace is to appear and the devastated life of the earth renew itself."

Buber returned to America in the spring of 1957 to give a series of lectures at the Washington School of Psychiatry. That year a book of his essays and lectures, from the early writings to the speeches given at Carnegie Hall and at the Paulskirche, was published in New York under the title *Pointing the Way*.

In February of the next year Martin Buber celebrated his eightieth birthday. Messages of congratulations and good wishes came from all over the world. His granddaughter put them in a large, attractive box which she set before him. There were so many he could not possibly answer them all, yet he wanted to express his thanks to each one. This he did with a printed card, directed, he said, not to a totality but to the individual. "The older one becomes, so much more grows in one the inclination to give thanks," he wrote. "Before all to

In this photograph taken at the Washington, D.C., School of Psychiatry in 1957, Buber has the look of a Biblical prophet. He was eighty years old at the time of the lectures. (WIDE WORLD PHOTOS)

what is above. Now, indeed, so strongly as could never have been possible before, life is felt as an unearned gift, and especially each hour that is entirely good one receives, like a surprising present, with outstretched thankful hands. But after that, it is necessary time and again to thank one's fellowman, even when he has not done anything especially for one. For what, then? For the fact that when he met me, he had really met me, that he opened his eyes and did not confuse me with anyone else, that he opened his ears and reliably heard what I had to say to him, yes, that he opened what I really addressed, his well-closed heart. . . ."

That spring found Buber back in the United States as guest lecturer at Princeton. While there he received a letter from Dag Hammarskjöld, then Secretary-General of the United Nations. He had read *Pointing the Way,* and had been deeply impressed, especially by the later speeches: "I want to tell you how strongly I have responded to what you write about our age of distrust and to the background of your observations which I find in your philosophy of unity created out of the manifold."

A few weeks after receiving the letter, Martin Buber visited the United Nations as Hammarskjöld's guest. The two men sat across from each other in the wood-paneled office of the secretary-general and talked of the concern both felt over the lack of trust among nations: "He who stood in the most exposed position of international responsibility, and I who stand in the loneliness of a spiritual tower, which is in reality a watchtower from which all the distances and depths of the planetary crisis can be descried," Buber said in describing their meeting.

They were disturbed alike by the way the representatives of the various nations, in their mutual distrust, talked past each other. Each hoped and believed that, before it was too late, true representatives of the nations would come forth, men faithful to their mission, and enter into genuine dialogue, for the common interests of the people were stronger than those that kept them apart.

Coexistence, a word often heard then, was not enough, the two men agreed. In spite of the overwhelming problems, cooperation was surely to be preferred over complete destruction and the end of all that was called civilization. There was no third choice.

"We both recognized, Dag Hammarskjöld and I, what it was essentially that bound us to each other," Buber said. "But I sensed, looking at and listening to him, something else that I could not explain to myself, something fateful that in some way was connected with his function in this world-hour."

Soon after this meeting Dag Hammarskjöld was in England to receive an honorary degree from Cambridge. His speech of thanks showed the influence of his talk with Martin Buber: "We meet in a time of peace when there is no peace, in a time of technical achievement which threatens its own masters with destruction."

He quoted a great deal from Buber's Carnegie Hall speech, explaining to his audience that Buber was one of the influential thinkers of his time. "I excuse myself for having quoted at such great length from this speech," he said. "I have done so because out of the depth of his feelings Martin Buber has found expressions which it would be vain of me to try to improve. If I have wanted on this occasion to draw attention to the troubles of our time to which the quoted words have given such an impelling expression, this is because it is in a basic way related to the tasks and spirit of an institution like this University."

At a press conference after Hammarskjöld's return to New York, he was questioned about the lengthy quotation from the philosopher Martin Buber. The interviewer said that he had noticed a tone of pessimism for the first time in the secretary-general's attitude. "You referred to a 'kind of despair of Western civilization'; and in concluding your speech you said that deep-rooted conflicts which have run their course all through history continue, and destructive forces which have always been with us make themselves felt in new forms. My question is: Are we to note here an outlook of pessimism so far as mankind and the future of the World Organization are concerned?"

"If you read the speech that way you go too far," Hammarskjöld replied. "First of all the despair I talked about was a despair I was criticizing. As you may have seen in the speech I said that I found the despair of Western civilization unjustified. . . . My fear is related to one single thing which I think has been brought out very well in the Buber statement—that is, the drift into what Buber called existential reciprocal mistrust."

The previous year and the year before that, Dag Hammarskjöld had flown to the Near East when trouble flared up between Israel and the neighboring countries. In Egypt he talked with Nasser and in Jerusalem with Ben-Gurion, who had come out of retirement and was again the prime minister. Both men had been stubborn. "We'll give two blows for one," Ben-Gurion had declared. And when it seemed that the negotiations were succeeding, Nasser siezed the Suez Canal and closed it to Israeli ships and all ships bound for Israel. In retaliation Israel sent 32,000 troops across the border into the Egyptian-held Sinai Peninsula. France and Britain, chief stockholders of the canal, joined Israel and sent invasion forces into Egypt. The United Nations, through Hammarskjöld, acted quickly to prevent another world war by bringing about a cease-fire and establishing an international police force to clear the canal and see to the evacuation of invading troops.

In 1959 Dag Hammarskjöld was back in the Near East on one of his many missions of peace, and in Jerusalem he called on Martin Buber. It was in January, the time of the year the Arabs call Spring of Winter, when the rains bring a brief but tender green cover to the hills, with splashes of bright flowers whose seeds have lain dormant during the dry summer. In the house of Lovers of Zion Street the world's problems could be forgotten for a little while. The two men talked about philosophy

Dag Hammarskjöld (right) visits Martin Buber in his home in Jerusalem in January 1959, while on a three-week trip to the Middle East. (CULVER PICTURES, INC.)

and the failure of spiritual man in his historical under-
takings. Buber pointed out Plato's attempt to establish
an ideal state in Sicily. Plato, observing that all states
were so poorly governed, came to the conclusion that
one of two things must be done to produce the right
leaders. Either the philosopher himself should rule, or
one whom he had taught to govern his life philosophi-
cally. "I felt, and Hammarskjöld—of that I was certain
—also felt as I did, we too were the recipients of that
letter in which Plato tells of his failure and of his overcoming his failure."

Paula Buber had died recently while they were in
Vienna, and there she was buried. Theirs had been a
marriage and close companionship for sixty years. For
his sake she had accepted exile. His people became her
people, and his God her God. Their older granddaughter, Barbara, and her husband and children were living
with him. She ran the household as her grandmother
had done, looking after the practical details, seeing to
his comfort, acting as hostess to his visitors, and cheer-
ing him in his loneliness.

In the spring of 1960 Theodor Heuss visited Israel.
When he lectured in Jerusalem, Martin Buber gave the
speech of welcome. His mind went back to the time they
had met before, when Heuss was president of the German Republic and Buber was given the Frankfurt
Peace Prize. With a note of tenderness he now spoke of
it: "And my heart still knows how, before I began to
speak I first looked at my wife—she who had instilled

the lasting presence of a genuine and free Germany into my life."

Buber spoke of that other Germany under the rule of Adolf Hitler, a subject uppermost in the minds of his listeners who had come to hear the first German of note to visit Israel since then. The antihuman wave that had surged up with the Nazis had its roots in the mistrust of men one against another, Buber said. And now from that there had arisen the reciprocal mistrust of nations.

The year before, soon after leaving office, Heuss had also been given the Peace Prize. In the course of his speech of thanks, he had said, "All my life I have been unable to bear the word 'tolerance.' " Buber reminded him of this, saying, "You have spoken my inmost thought. Nothing can be accomplished when men merely try to put up with each other. Nothing merely willed, such as allowing one another to exist, can help. Only something that has grown." Heuss had made another remark earlier, when he had received the Hanseatic Goethe Prize, and this too Buber quoted. He had spoken of that human trust that grows in the depths as the presupposition of a democratic form of life. "But it is also the presupposition of a genuine dialogue that is being opened up between two democracies," Buber added. "We sons of a younger democracy, which knows itself, however, as the heir of ancient promises and biddings, would harken to your words about the self-formations of democracy as the beginning of such a dialogue."

Martin Buber had often been spoken of as a possible

candidate for the Nobel Prize in literature. In 1949, the year the Prize went to William Faulkner, he had been nominated by Hermann Hesse, who said of him, "Martin Buber is in my judgment not only one of the few wise men who live on earth at the present time, he is also a writer of a very high order and, more than that, he has enriched world literature with a genuine treasure as has no other living author—the tales of the Hasidim."

Dag Hammarskjöld also had plans to submit his name. In August 1961 he wrote to Buber, telling him again how he was impressed by his philosophy. "I would like to translate some of these books into Swedish so as to bring you closer to my countrymen," he said, and he asked which book Buber thought the most suitable. In his reply Buber suggested *I and Thou*.

A month later, on September 18, Buber heard over the radio the news that shocked the world. Dag Hammarskjöld had been killed in a plane crash in northern Rhodesia while seeking a cease-fire between UN forces and Katanga forces in the Congo. Only an hour after hearing this, a letter was brought to Buber. It was from Hammarskjöld, saying that he had gone to work on the translation immediately. This book was a key work, he said, and decisive in its message. Later it was learned that in the briefcase he had taken on that fateful trip was a copy of *I and Thou* and the first ten pages of his translation.

At eighty-three so many of one's friends live only in memory. Once, when Buber was young and death seemed far away, he had answered a circulated question about a belief in life after death: "To wish to extend our conception beyond death, to wish to anticipate in the soul what death alone can reveal to us in existence, seems to me to be a lack of faith clothed as faith. The genuine faith speaks: I know nothing of death, but I know that God is eternity, and I know this too, that He is my God. Whether what we call time remains to us beyond our death becomes quite unimportant to us next to this knowing, that we are God's—who is not immortal, but eternal."

Three of Paula Buber's books were brought out in one volume in 1961, under the title *Spirits and Men*. "They are not fairy tales," Buber wrote in the foreword, "not romantic ghost stories, but genuine tales of spirits, reports of them, of spirits which in a special kind of natural mystery enter into our lives and perhaps abandon themselves to them." Two years later he wrote a foreword for the collected works of his son-in-law Ludwig Strauss, who had died in 1953.

On his eighty-fifth birthday Buber again wrote a printed reply of thanks for the many messages of congratulations. He reflected on the word *to thank*. In German and in English it is associated with *think,* in the sense of to *think of,* to *remember.* To say *thank you* means also I will hold you in memory—a joyous, friendly memory. The word in Hebrew, *hodoth,* means, first, to *avow faith* (*in someone*), that is, to confirm him in his existence. So, in his reply, Buber wrote that he held in grateful memory and confirmed each person whose good wishes he had received on his birthday.

Buber (at right) is pictured with Hebrew University scholars who visited him at his home in Jerusalem on February 8, 1963, to celebrate his eighty-fifth birthday. (WIDE WORLD PHOTOS)

178 MARTIN BUBER: *Wisdom in Our Time*

Honors continued to come to him, though he at-
tached little importance to them. He often quoted the
advice one of the Hasidic masters had given his disciples. A man should have two pockets to reach into according to the need, in the right one the words "For my
sake the world was created," and in the left, "I am but
dust and ashes." Dag Hammarskjöld's death had pre-
vented Buber's receiving the Nobel Prize in 1961, but in
1963, the year that he was eighty-five, he received an
honor that ranked as high in Europe, the Erasmus
Award, given for one who has contributed to the spiritual unity of Europe. He flew from Israel to Holland,
the country where the great humanist Erasmus, for
whom the prize was named, had lived five hundred
years earlier. At the ceremony in Amsterdam he was
cited for enriching the spiritual life of Europe with his
versatile gifts for more than half a century, and he was
credited with freeing from misconceptions and prejudices the contact between Judaism, on the one hand,
and belief in the Bible and modern culture on the other.
When Buber gave his speech of thanks to His Royal
Highness Prince Bernhard and to the members of the
prize committee, his eyes, through habit, must have
searched the audience for Paula, and surely he felt the
presence of her spirit with him. The next year he was
back in Europe to accept an honorary doctorate from
the University of Heidelberg.

He was growing frail now, and the travels away from
Israel soon came to an end. The days passed gently.
Every afternoon, after the siesta, he went out for a

walk, accompanied by his granddaughter Barbara. They turned to the right, and at the cross street they turned again to the right, where they came to a small park. There they sat on a bench to rest. Olive trees so old they seemed to have been part of Creation shaded them. Sometimes flocks of chubby jays, almost tame compared to the European jays, gathered in noisy flocks on the electric wires. Cats, sunning themselves on every garden wall and balcony, blinked lazily, like so many Egyptian goddesses, and took no notice of the birds.

The granddaughter tried to protect Martin Buber from the demands on his time, but when she wanted to limit his callers, he said, "If they seek me out, I must see them." Many of the world's great who visited Israel called on him. And, as always, there were the students. Buber especially enjoyed talking with the young. Once he wrote that if he had been asked when he was young whether he preferred books or men, he would have chosen books. But as he grew older he enjoyed being with people. "He loved to talk," it was said of him. "But he could listen best of all."

At the end of May still another honor came to Martin Buber. He was given the Freedom of Jerusalem Award as one of the greatest Jewish thinkers and humanists. By then his great strength had failed. He was confined to his bed following surgery for leg fracture. Two weeks after receiving the award, he died while in a coma. "The end is already to be found in the beginning, and in the end is a new beginning."

One who knew him had written, "If we find the heart

of existentialism in the protest against systems, con-
cepts and abstractions, and above all in the challenge of
human existence, then one might well conclude there is
in reality only one existentialist, Martin Buber, and he
is no existentialist."

BIBLIOGRAPHY

Cohen, Arthur. MARTIN BUBER. London: Bowes and Bowes. 1957.

Diamond, Malcolm L. MARTIN BUBER: *Jewish Existentialist*. New York: Oxford University Press. 1960.

Friedman, Maurice S. MARTIN BUBER: *The Life of Dialogue*. New York: Harper & Row. 1960.

Rosenzweig, Franz. ON JEWISH LEARNING. Edited by Nahum N. Glatzer. New York: Schocken Books Inc. 1955.

————. FRANZ ROSENZWEIG: *His Life and Thoughts*. Edited by Nahum N. Glatzer. New York: Schocken Books Inc. 1953.

Fleg, Edmond, ed. THE JEWISH ANTHOLOGY. New York: Harcourt Brace Co. 1925.

Buber, Martin. THE TALES OF RABBI NACHMAN. Bloomington: Indiana University Press. 1962.

————. JEWISH MYSTICISM AND THE LEGENDS OF BAALSHEM. London: J. M. Dent & Sons, Ltd. 1931.

————. TALES OF THE HASIDIM: *Early Masters*. New York: Schocken Books Inc. 1947.

————. TALES OF THE HASIDIM: *Later Masters*. New York: Schocken Books Inc. 1948.

————. TEN RUNGS: *Hasidic Sayings*. New York: Schocken Books Inc. 1947.

————. THE PROPHETIC FAITH. New York: Macmillan Co. 1949.

————. MOSES: *The Revelation and the Covenant*. New York: Harper & Row. 1958.

————. BETWEEN MAN AND MAN. London: Kegan, Paul, Trench, Trubner & Co., Ltd. 1947.

————. ISRAEL AND THE WORLD: *Essays in a Time of Crisis*. New York: Schocken Books Inc. 1948.

————. PATHS IN UTOPIA. New York: Macmillan Co. 1950.

————. TWO TYPES OF FAITH: *A Study of the Interpenetration of Judaism and Christianity*. New York: Macmillan Co. 1951.

————. GOOD AND EVIL: *Two Interpretations*. New York: Charles Scribner's Sons. 1953.

————. ECLIPSE OF GOD: *A Critique of the Key Twentieth-century Philosophies*. New York: Harper & Row. 1952.

————. I AND THOU. 2nd ed. New York: Charles Scribner's Sons. 1958.

————. POINTING THE WAY. Collected Essays. New York: Harper & Row. 1957.

————. THE KNOWLEDGE OF MAN: *Selected Essays.* New York: Harper & Row. 1965.

————. A BELIEVING HUMANISM: *My Testament 1902–1965.* New York: Simon and Schuster. 1967.

INDEX

185